Sweeter than Chocolate!®

Sweet Words and Real Solutions from God's Book

An Inductive Study of Psalm 119

by

pam gillaspie

Dedicated with love to . . .

Mom and Dad for always loving me unconditionally and raising me to know God's truth.

Precept Ministries and Kay for helping me to discover my spiritual gifts and equipping me to go forth and serve others.

Jan for generously pouring out wisdom and encouraging me to fully live out God's calling on my life.

Acknowledgments

Thanks to my dear husband Dave for the cover and layout design. Could God have given me a more perfect match? I don't think so.

Cress, Mary Ann, and Susan, thank you so much for your help in proofreading. You have freed me to study and write when I would have been obsessing over semi-colon usage.

John, thank you for believing in this project. Your enthusiasm spurs me on. Thank you Jan for continuing to "run things up the flagpole." Rick, thanks for your red pen—your edits and questions have brought clarity.

My dear Bible study ladies, thank you for coming along on this adventure. You are dearer to me than you can imagine.

Scripture taken from the NEW AMERICAN STANDARD BIBLE®,
© Copyright 1960, 1962, 1963, 1968, 1971, 1972, 1973, 1975, 1977, 1995 by The Lockman Foundation.
Used by permission. (www.Lockman.org)

Precept, Precept Ministries International, Precept Ministries International the Inductive Bible Study People, the Plumb Bob design, Precept Upon Precept, In & Out, Sweeter than Chocolate!®, Cookies on the Lower Shelf, Precepts For Life, Precepts From God's Word and Transform Student Ministries are trademarks of Precept Ministries International.

Sweeter than Chocolate!®

Copyright © 2009 by Pam Gillaspie
Published by Precept Ministries International
P.O. Box 182218
Chattanooga, Tennessee 37422
www.precept.org

ISBN 978-1-934884-79-9

Printed in the United States of America

2012

Sweeter than **Chocolate!**®

Sweet Words and Real Solutions from God's Book

An Inductive Study of Psalm 119

There is nothing quite like your favorite pair of jeans. You can dress them up, you can dress them down. You can work in them, play in them, shop in them . . . live in them. They always feel right. It is my hope that the structure of this Bible study will fit you like those jeans; that it will work with your life right now, right where you are whether you're new to this whole Bible thing or whether you've been studying the Book for years!

How could that even be possible? Smoke and mirrors, perhaps? The new mercilessly thrown in the deep end of exegesis or the experienced given pom-poms and the job of simply cheering others on? None of the above.

Sweeter than Chocolate!® is designed with options that will allow you to go as deep each week as you desire. If you're just starting out and feeling a little overwhelmed, stick with the main text and don't think a second thought about the sidebar assignments. If you're looking for a challenge, then take the sidebar prompts and go ahead and dig all the way to China! As you move along through the study, think of the sidebars and "Digging Deeper" boxes as that 2% of lycra that you find in certain jeans . . . the wiggle-room that will help them fit just right.

Beginners may find that they want to start adding in some of the optional assignments as they go along. The experts may find that when three children are throwing up for three days straight, foregoing those assignments for the week would be the way to live wisely.

Life has a way of ebbing and flowing and this study is designed to ebb and flow right along with it!

Enjoy!

How to use this study

Sweeter than Chocolate!® studies meet you where you are and take you as far as you want to go.

1. WEEKLY STUDY: The main text guides you through the complete topic of study for the week.

2. FYI boxes: For Your Information boxes provide bite-sized material to shed additional light on the topic.

FYI:

Reading Tip: Begin with Prayer

You may have heard this a million times over and if this is a million and one, so be it. Whenever you read or study God's Word, first pray and ask His Spirit to be your Guide.

3. ONE STEP FURTHER and other sidebar boxes: Sidebar boxes give you the option to push yourself a little further. If you have extra time or are looking for an extra challenge, you can try one, all, or any number in between! These boxes give you the ultimate in flexibility.

ONE STEP FURTHER:

Word Study: *torah* / law

The first of eight Hebrew key words we encounter for God's Word is *torah* translated "law." If you're up for a challenge this week, do a word study to learn what you can about *torah*. Run a concordance search and examine where the word *torah* appears in the Old Testament and see what you can learn about from the contexts.

If you decide to look for the word for "law" in the New Testament, you'll find that the primary Greek word is *nomos*.

Be sure to see what Paul says about the law in Galatians 3 and what Jesus says in Matthew 5.

4. DIGGING DEEPER boxes: If you're looking to go further, Digging Deeper sections will help you sharpen your skills as you continue to mine the truths of Scripture for yourself.

Digging Deeper

What else does God's Word say about counselors?

If you can, spend some time this week digging around for what God's Word says about counselors.

Start by considering what you already know about counsel from the Word of God and see if you can show where these truths are in the Bible. Make sure that the Word actually says what you think it says.

Week One
Taste and See!

Aleph

How sweet are Your words to my taste!
Yes, sweeter than honey to my mouth!
—*Psalm 119:103*

Is the Bible really the best thing since sliced bread? Is it better than chocolate, more valuable than the fastest rising stock around, more effective than the planet's best GPS? In our language, those are the claims it makes about itself. *But is it what it says it is?*

The fact that the Bible is not only the best selling book of all time, but also the best selling book *every year* suggests that Americans support this view—at least with their wallets. As we begin our inductive study of Psalm 119, we need to take a step back and examine the landscape of our views about God's Word, our culture's view of it, and the claims that the Bible makes about itself. If God's Word really is what it claims to be; if it really does what it claims to do; and if you choose to align your life with its claims, it could change your life forever. It has changed mine!

While we will explore the text from many angles asking many questions of it as we go, the questions that must remain in the forefront, the questions that at the end of the day will make all the difference are these: *Is the Bible actually what it claims to be? Does the Bible actually do what it claims to do?*

If the answers are yes, we are fools if we don't align ourselves accordingly with its truths. If the answers are no, we are fools if we bother.

It is that simple.

So, grab a pencil and a piece of chocolate (I'm serious about this) and let's get started!

FYI:

If You're in a Class
Complete **Week One** together on your first day of class. This will be a great way to start getting to know one another and will help those who are newer to Bible study get their bearings.

CONSIDER the WAY you THINK

What do you know about the claims the Bible makes about itself?

ONE STEP FURTHER:

Study Tip: Running a Concordance Search

If you're not sure what claims the Bible makes about itself, you might consider running a concordance search. A Bible concordance is simply an alphabetical listing of all of the words that appear in the text of the Bible. In running a concordance search on this topic, some words and phrases that might yield helpful results are "Your word," "My word," and "scripture." The more you search, the more you will get the feel for how to do it, just like with Googling topics online. What are other possible search words or phrases that might help you discover what the Bible says about itself?

What are your views about the Bible? What kind of role has it played in your life?

How do your personal views about and/or experiences with the Bible line up with the claims it makes about itself? Are they congruent or is there a degree of disconnection? Why do you think this is?

FYI:

Study Tip: Online Tools

Using a concordance is a fast and painless process with the Internet. Check out www.blueletterbible.org or www.crosswalk.com for free online Bible study tools.

OBSERVE the TEXT of SCRIPTURE

READ through the entire text of Psalm 119 and jot down briefly some of the benefits that the psalmist says come from God's Word. We are taking a quick overview right now, so keep your zeal in check and don't write down more than one benefit per stanza. Note as you read that the psalmist uses a number of synonyms for God's Word.

What are some of the synonyms for God's Word?

REASON through the IMPLICATIONS

Considering what you have seen in Psalm 119, how do its claims line up with your life experience? For instance, *Have you found God's Word to be a delight? Have you found God's Word to be a counselor?* etc.

ONE STEP FURTHER:

Thinking Ahead

What might be important questions to ask regarding the background of the Psalm and its context within Scripture? You'll find some questions on the following pages, but before you turn there take a little time to think what they might be. Keep thinking ahead. Anticipate questions, think about other verses that might be relevant, consider other places in Scripture that might shed light on the passage that you are studying. Where else would you dig if all you had in front of you was the text of Scripture? As you contemplate some of the possible questions, consider where you can find the answers.

Notes

WHERE WE ARE . . .

A LOOK at the STATS

excerpted from www.theologicalstudies.org

"Most Americans own a Bible. In fact, 92% of households in America own at least one copy. Of those households that own a Bible, the average number of Bibles is three. This includes not only the homes of practicing Christians but hundreds of thousands of atheists as well.

"Although most Americans own a Bible, use of the Bible varies significantly. In a poll taken by the Gallup Organization in October, 2000, 59% of Americans reported that they read the Bible at least occasionally. This is down from 73% in the 1980s. The percentage of Americans who read the Bible at least once a week is 37%. This is down slightly from 40% in 1990. According to the Barna Research Group [1997 data], those who read the Bible regularly spend about 52 minutes a week in the Scriptures." [1]

REASONING through the NUMBERS

Fifty-two minutes a week in the Scriptures might not seem that bad, but let's stop and do some math here. If a person spends 52 minutes a week in the Bible, how much time is that each day? About seven and a half minutes, less time than a person spends watching commercials in an average 30-minute television show.

Even more disturbing is the fact that people tend to make themselves look better to pollsters than they really are, overreporting such things as how often they vote and how much they give to charity and underreporting such things as illegal drug use.

Given this tendency, the amount of time spent reading the Bible on an average day among people who call themselves "Bible readers" may very well be closer to five minutes.

Think for a bit about how much time you invest in your significant relationships. What would your relationships with your spouse, your children, your friends (or even your dog for that matter) be if you only gave them five minutes a day?

These statistics suggest that the vast majority of the visible church (to say nothing of those outside) is in the Word of God marginally at best.

Perhaps many today who have doubts that God's Word is what it says it is have just not given it a chance.

Christianity, if you boil it all the way down, centers on one question: *Is Jesus who He says He is?*

This study, as mentioned, focuses on a related question: *Is the Bible all that it says it is?*

Certainly there are those who already believe that the Bible is what it says it is and does what it says it does. In this study, you will learn more about its benefits.

For skeptics the invitation is as clear as Jesus made it to those He walked with: "Come and see." He didn't ask for blind faith. He invited people to check things out for themselves.

ONE STEP FURTHER:

Blazing the Trail

If you're up for a real challenge this week, consider questions that may need to be answered regarding the background and context of this chapter and list them in your "Notes" section. Then, research answers and also identify potential issues in the text. Remember, this is an optional assignment to keep those who are up for a serious challenge engaged.

The psalmist boldly asserts that God's Word is sweet to the taste, likening it to honey. He writes not only the longest psalm by far at 176 verses, but also the longest single chapter in the Bible as he speaks of the truths and benefits of God's Word from a myriad of angles. Before we dive into the text more closely, though, we need to consider a bit of the background and context of this monumental piece of Scripture.

BACKGROUND INFORMATION

Psalm 119 is an acrostic poem comprised of 22 stanzas based on the 22-letter Hebrew alphabet. Each stanza has eight lines, each beginning with the respective letter of the Hebrew alphabet. If we were to compose a comparable poem in English, ours would have 26 stanzas. In the first eight-line stanza, each line would begin with the letter A. In the second stanza, each of the eight lines would begin with the letter B and so on through the entire alphabet.

QUESTIONS of AUTHORSHIP and DATE

In addition to understanding the genre of the literature, other questions we commonly want answered when we begin to study a passage of Scripture concern authorship and dating.

Who wrote it? and When was it written? We can gather some information on these topics by observing the text. That said, however, this is one of the areas where we often find ourselves needing the input of the experts. Scholars can help us wade through issues not readily apparent to us by simply reading the text. The experts, though, will nearly always have varied opinions so there's a sense in which we need to become experts in learning how to utilize the experts! If you're feeling confused right about now, take a deep breath and relax.

So how do we become experts at evaluating the experts, or to put it in other words, at discerning which expert has the truth?

First, make sure that you are soaking yourself both in the text at hand and in the Word of God in general. A great temptation in studying God's Word is to put down the Bible and overuse commentaries and comments scholars have made about it instead of letting the Holy Spirit guide into all truth. There is, perhaps, no graver error we can make. Scholars are important, but they're not inspired. The power is in the Word, not academic tomes.

Second, if you find that you need some help understanding part of a text, don't rely on the opinion of just one scholar or book. The best commentaries lay out various opinions on texts or topics and then tell you why the authors chose the position they hold. You can then find the scholars who hold the opposing views and compare both with the Word to see which arguments hold the most weight.

ONE STEP FURTHER:

Why not?
Why not try and learn the Hebrew alphabet as we go along? In order to help us to that end, we'll refer to each stanza by its name from the Hebrew alphabet in addition to using the verse numbers we're accustomed to.

If you already set out to answer the question of authorship and dating on your own, you probably discovered that scholars disagree on both.

While many Psalms come with what journalists call a byline (a clear statement of who wrote the Psalm), sometimes even including bonus information on the event it was written for, Psalm 119 is often referred to as an orphan Psalm because there is no claim of authorship attached to it.

Not surprisingly, then, a variety of opinions regarding who penned this master-piece of Hebrew literature and when have surfaced.

SO WHO WROTE PSALM 119?

The short answer is this: Scripture does not tell us. The name historically attached to the Psalm by the Jewish rabbis is King David, and much in the content and style of the text suggests that this is a good hypothesis. Other scholars have suggested that it was penned by Ezra the scribe as the people were reestablishing temple worship in Jerusalem after the period of exile. You can see how the issue of authorship and date are tied together. If David is the author, the date is much earlier than the date for Ezra. Because Scripture is silent on the author, we need to hold our opinions loosely. As you read, though, consider whether or not the Psalm has the same feel as other Davidic work. Consider whether the content is consistent with David's thinking or someone else's. In 119:23, for instance, the author makes reference to princes sitting around and talking about him. This is something David, and perhaps not a lot of other people, could have said. Watch for examples like this in the text that may hint at authorship.

OBSERVE the TEXT of SCRIPTURE

READ the Aleph stanza (Psalm 119:1-8) and mark every word and synonym that refers to God's Word.

Aleph

1   How blessed are those whose way is blameless, who walk in the law of the LORD.

2   How blessed are those who observe His testimonies, who seek Him with all their *heart*.

3   They also do no unrighteousness; they walk in His ways.

4   You have ordained Your precepts, that we should keep them *diligently*.

5   Oh that my ways may be established to keep Your statutes!

6   Then I shall not be ashamed when I look upon all Your commandments.

7   I shall give thanks to You with uprightness of heart, when I learn Your righteous judgments.

8   I shall keep Your statutes; do not forsake me utterly!

FYI:

Marking the Text
While you can mark the text any way that makes sense to you, here is a suggested way to mark the *Word of God* in this Psalm.

Try using a yellow colored pencil to mark synonyms for God's Word. As you identify specific Hebrew words, you can use a different colored pencil or pen to make a box around the outside of the words.

For example:
References to *law* can be yellow outlined in blue. References to God's *precepts* can be yellow outlined in green. By doing this, you will see how often synonyms for God's Word appear as well as their diversity.

DISCUSS with your GROUP or PONDER on your own . . .

What words in the Aleph stanza are synonyms for God's Word?

Do you notice any general pattern in their placement?

Who is being talked about in the Aleph stanza? Is there a shift at any point? If so, identify where it occurs and describe it.

Digging Deeper

Basics of a Word Study: Blameless

Doing a word study on *blameless* will yield some very interesting results. If you have the time, let's work through this one together.

Search on the Hebrew word from the text of Psalm 119:1 and note contexts in which this word is typically used.

If you're using *blueletterbible.org* you can take the following steps:

1. **Type in Psalm 119:1.** Change the version to NASB. **Click the "Search" button.**

2. When you arrive at the next screen, you will see six lettered boxes to the left of Psalm 119:1.
   Click the "C" button to take you to the concordance link.

3. **Click on the Strong's number,** in this case 8549, which is the link to the original word in Hebrew. Clicking this number will bring up another screen that will give you a brief definition of the word as well as list every occurrence of that particular Hebrew word in the Old Testament.

Before running to the dictionary definition, scan places where this word is used in Scripture. Examine the general contexts where it is used.

Interestingly, by far the greatest use of this word has to do with an undefiled sacrifice, a sacrifice acceptable to God. The highest volume of occurrences is in books that spell out how to keep the Law.

Are any people described as blameless? What can you find out about them? Did they live before or after the Law? Does this make a difference? Why or why not?

FYI:

Key Words in Psalm 119

In the text of Psalm 119, eight key Hebrew words refer to God's Word. Two other words translated "way" are also important but occur a little less frequently.

Mercifully, the translators of the NASB have translated the words consistently so the only time we will question what Hebrew word we are dealing with will come up when we encounter the words "word" (either *dabar* or *imrah*) and "way" (either *derek* or *orach*). As we move through our study we'll look at each of the words.

Key Words:

Law (*torah*)

Testimonies (*edah*)

Precepts (*piqqud*)

Statutes (*choq*)

Commandments (*mitsvah*)

Ordinances [also translated judgments] (*mishpat*)

Word (*dabar*)

Word (*imrah*)

Bonus Words:

Way (*derek*)

Way (*orach*)

If you have access to other study tools, you may want to check resources like the *Theological Wordbook of the Old Testament* for other scholarly inputs. Record your findings.

Search for *blameless* in the New Testament and see what you discover.

Focusing on verses 1-4, describe the person the psalmist calls blessed. What does this person do? Why and how does he do it? As you respond, quote directly from the text.

In verse 5, what does the psalmist ask of God for himself?

ONE STEP FURTHER:

Word Study: *torah* / law

The first of eight Hebrew key words we encounter for God's Word is *torah* translated "law." If you're up for a challenge this week, do a word study to learn what you can about *torah*. Run a concordance search and examine where the word *torah* appears in the Old Testament and see what you can learn about from the contexts.

If you decide to look for the word for "law" in the New Testament, you'll find that the primary Greek word is *nomos*.

Be sure to see what Paul says about the law in Galatians 3 and what Jesus says in Matthew 5.

TRUE STORIES:

Noah and Job

The two most notable stories we have of people who are referred to as blameless are Noah and Job. Noah's story appears in Genesis 6-9, while Job's appears in the book bearing his name. If you are looking for some additional reading, either story will give you a look into the life of a man who was walking in a manner pleasing to God. Both of them lived before the giving of the Law. Although they are called blameless, we know from the full context of Scripture that there is none who is without sin and that it is through the perfect sacrifice of Christ that we will one day be presented before God as "holy and blameless and beyond reproach" as Paul tells us in Colossians 1:22.

Week One: **Taste and See!**

In the remaining part of the Aleph stanza, what benefits does the psalmist look forward to as a result of keeping God's statutes?

FYI:

Asking Questions of the Text

The key to exegesis (that's the fancy word meaning to draw meaning out of Scripture) is asking questions of the text. The basic investigative questions Who? What? When? Where? Why? and How? will be your framework. Not every question can be addressed to every verse, and some verses require several variations on the same question. As we study Psalm 119 together, realize that not every question that can be asked will be asked, but don't let that stop you from asking other questions and exploring further on your own. We will never run out of questions to ask and answers to glean from God's Word!

What does the Aleph stanza teach us about God?

Does anything in the text bother you? If so, you have a clue that you need to either ask more questions, start applying, or both. Sometimes we are bothered because we have not studied and understood the text fully. Other times we are bothered because we have fully understood and simply don't want to accept or obey. Either way, when a text bothers us, it requires more attention.

Record below anything that is still bothering you within the text, as well as some questions you can ask and strategies you can take to answer the questions. In a little bit, we will look at a potentially bothersome spot together and see what we can discover simply by studying thoroughly.

Digging Deeper

Examining a Perplexing Phrase

What is up with the prayer "Do not forsake me utterly!"? Doesn't it say somewhere else in the Bible that God will never leave us or forsake us? At face value, this phrase may seem to contradict that. So what do we do with it? It's in the text so we can't just ignore it.

Certainly the easiest approach is to run to a commentary. However, you'll find that there aren't a lot of commentaries that deal line by line with Psalm 119. Even if they did, you'd still have to discern whether or not you agreed with the commentator. Remember, commentaries are helpful. Scholars often ask questions lay people would never think to raise. Still, you'll want to seek that input after you have first wrestled with the text yourself.

Here is an approach for working through this prayer:

—Consider what you have already learned about the context in which the phrase occurs. What are the repeated words or concepts?

—What did you learn from studying the words *torah* and *blameless*? What do they tell you about the context of this phrase?

The psalmist has the Law of God in the front of his mind as he is penning this psalm. Understanding this context is crucial for helping us understand some of the concepts in the text.

As you may have discovered in your research this week, the Law and the covenant into which Israel entered with God held out both a blessing and a curse. The people would be blessed if they kept the covenant, but they would be cursed if they broke it. This is a foreign idea to many people who have read only the New Testament, but it is entirely biblical. If you have time, it is a great idea for you to take a few minutes and read through Deuteronomy 11 and 27–31. In Deuteronomy 11 we have a clear statement about the blessing and curse.

Deuteronomy 11:26-28

26 *"See, I am setting before you today a blessing and a curse:*

27 *the blessing, if you listen to the commandments of the LORD your God, which I am commanding you today;*

28 *and the curse, if you do not listen to the commandments of the LORD your God, but turn aside from the way which I am commanding you today, by following other gods which you have not known."*

In Deuteronomy 27–31 Moses addresses the children of Israel standing at the border of the promised land and passes the baton of leadership to Joshua. Again we see as part of the covenant, if the people forsake God, He will forsake them.

Deuteronomy 31:14-18

14 *Then the LORD said to Moses, "Behold, the time for you to die is near; call Joshua, and present yourselves at the tent of meeting, that I may commission him." So Moses and Joshua went and presented themselves at the tent of meeting.*

15 *The LORD appeared in the tent in a pillar of cloud, and the pillar of cloud stood at the doorway of the tent.*

16 *The LORD said to Moses, "Behold, you are about to lie down with your fathers; and this people will arise and play the harlot with the strange gods of the land, into the midst of which they are going, and will forsake Me and break My covenant which I have made with them.*

17 *"Then My anger will be kindled against them in that day, and I will forsake them and hide My face from them, and they will be consumed, and many evils and troubles will come upon them; so that they will say in that day, 'Is it not because our God is not among us that these evils have come upon us?'*

18 *"But I will surely hide My face in that day because of all the evil which they will do, for they will turn to other gods."*

The psalmist knew the Law. He knew the covenant required obedience and that God was looking for His people to follow Him in obedience. When the psalmist says, "Do not forsake me utterly," he is asking God to keep His end of the covenant. The psalmist plans to keep God's statutes and when he does, God will not forsake him.

REASON THROUGH THE TEXT

How does this view of covenant fit in with what you know of the Bible at this point?

Does this imply that we are made right through works? Why or why not?

If you have not read Matthew 5 and Galatians 3, take some time and do that now, noting what Jesus and Paul say about the Law. Does this impact the response you gave above?

Remember, we are looking at an Old Testament text and God revealed His truth to man progressively. As Paul tells us in Galatians, the purpose of the Law was not to make us righteous, but to show us our imperfection to lead us to Christ who is the fulfillment of the Law. We have power to obey because He dwells within us!

Week One: **Taste and See!**

ANYTHING ELSE . . .

Use this space to jot down anything else from this stanza that you might want to go back and investigate more thoroughly in the future.

@THE END OF THE DAY . . .

What have you learned from the text this week that you can apply to your life?

What would a life without shame mean to people today who often live steeped in it?

How does your love for God's Word compare with that of the psalmist?

As you close out your study this week, take some quiet time (perhaps 30 minutes to an hour) to simply take a walk and quietly reflect on what you have learned. When you finish, write down any new thoughts God brought to your mind from His Word.

ONE STEP FURTHER:

Want to be a psalmist?

Here is an optional assignment that will help secure your understanding of the basic form of the Psalm and probably increase greatly your respect for its author. Following the pattern, write one sentence that relates to the truth or benefits of God's Word. As you do this, bear in mind that the Psalmist wrote eight sentences per stanza. Additionally, he was working in specific words and was doing a lot with syllable counts and parallelisms that we are not *even* going to get into!

Try it for yourself. Here, I'll get you started.

All of Your words are true.

Better than food to my body are Your precepts for life.

C

D

E

F

G

H

I

J

K

L

M

N

O

P

Q

R

S

T

U

V

W

X

Y

Z

Week One: **Taste and See!**

Week Two

Your Source for Answers in a World of Questions

בְּ   גּ   דּ   הּ

Beth   Gimel   Daleth   He

As we look at Psalm 119 this week, we will examine the next four stanzas, Beth, Gimel, Daleth, and He, as well as go back and review a little on Aleph. Reviewing and remembering are key when it comes to studying God's Word. Don't forget that the sidebars are provided to give you additional information and challenges. By sticking to the main text, you'll gain a solid overview of the Psalm that we're studying. You can add in the other material as much or as little as you like. And for those of you who are "study animals," who assume that the lesson is not done unless you've interacted with every last box, remember that there are weeks when you will not have as much time. Please use the optional assignments to give you the grace to breathe when you need it.

AN OVERVIEW OF THE TEXT

OBSERVE the TEXT of SCRIPTURE

Bet you thought that we were going to read through the entire Psalm again, didn't you?! Relax. Our overview today will focus only on the first five stanzas.

READ Psalm 119:1-40 and consider the questions that follow the text. Don't be overly concerned with whether you have seen the "right" things or asked the "right" questions. Many questions can be asked of any text. Part of good Bible study is simply *learning to ask questions* of the text. The more questions you ask, the more you will learn which ones have the most relevance. So, with that, pick up your pencils and have at it.

Aleph

1   *How blessed are those whose way is blameless, who walk in the law of the LORD.*

2   *How blessed are those who observe His testimonies, who seek Him with all their heart.*

3   *They also do no unrighteousness; they walk in His ways.*

4   *You have ordained Your precepts, that we should keep them diligently.*

5   *Oh that my ways may be established to keep Your statutes!*

6   *Then I shall not be ashamed when I look upon all Your commandments.*

7   *I shall give thanks to You with uprightness of heart, when I learn Your righteous judgments.*

8   *I shall keep Your statutes; do not forsake me utterly!*

Beth

9   *How can a young man keep his way pure? By keeping it according to Your word.*

10   *With all my heart I have sought You; do not let me wander from Your commandments.*

11   *Your word I have treasured in my heart, that I may not sin against You.*

12   *Blessed are You, O LORD; teach me Your statutes.*

13   *With my lips I have told of all the ordinances of Your mouth.*

14   *I have rejoiced in the way of Your testimonies, as much as in all riches.*

15   *I will meditate on Your precepts and regard Your ways.*

16   *I shall delight in Your statutes; I shall not forget Your word.*

Gimel

17   *Deal bountifully with Your servant, that I may live and keep Your word.*

18   *Open my eyes, that I may behold wonderful things from Your law.*

19   *I am a stranger in the earth; do not hide Your commandments from me.*

20   *My soul is crushed with longing after Your ordinances at all times.*

21   *You rebuke the arrogant, the cursed, who wander from Your commandments.*

22   *Take away reproach and contempt from me, for I observe Your testimonies.*

23   *Even though princes sit and talk against me, Your servant meditates on Your statutes.*

24   *Your testimonies also are my delight; they are my counselors.*

Daleth

25 My soul cleaves to the dust; revive me according to Your word.

26 I have told of my ways, and You have answered me; teach me Your statutes.

27 Make me understand the way of Your precepts, so I will meditate on Your wonders.

28 My soul weeps because of grief; strengthen me according to Your word.

29 Remove the false way from me, and graciously grant me Your law.

30 I have chosen the faithful way; I have placed Your ordinances before me.

31 I cling to Your testimonies; O LORD, do not put me to shame!

32 I shall run the way of Your commandments, for You will enlarge my heart.

He

33 Teach me, O LORD, the way of Your statutes, and I shall observe it to the end.

34 Give me understanding, that I may observe Your law and keep it with all my heart.

35 Make me walk in the path of Your commandments, for I delight in it.

36 Incline my heart to Your testimonies and not to dishonest gain.

37 Turn away my eyes from looking at vanity, and revive me in Your ways.

38 Establish Your word to Your servant, as that which produces reverence for You.

39 Turn away my reproach which I dread, for Your ordinances are good.

40 Behold, I long for Your precepts; revive me through Your righteousness.

FYI:

Reading Tip: Begin with Prayer

You may have heard this a million times over and if this is a million and one, so be it. Whenever you read or study God's Word, first pray and ask His Spirit to be your Guide.

Sweeter than Chocolate!®

An Inductive Study of Psalm 119

Week Two: **Your Source for Answers in a World of Questions**

DISCUSS with your GROUP or PONDER on your own . . .

What are your initial observations on the text?

What questions surface in your mind?

What words or phrases might you focus on for further study?

What is the biggest takeaway that you remember from last week? Do you see any tie-ins with what you've read so far in the text this week?

OBSERVE the TEXT of SCRIPTURE

READ Aleph through He (Psalm 119:1-40) again. This time examine what the psalmist prays for himself. As you do, note both what he wants and what he doesn't want. List your findings below. [If it helps, you can make a simple list of his requests. Then, go back and highlight the positive ones in one color and the negative in another.]

For example, in the Beth stanza the psalmist prays that he will not wander (negative) and that God will teach him His statutes (positive).

119:10b   Do not let me wander from Your commandments. (negative)

119:12b   Teach me Your statutes. (positive)

Looking over the list that you've compiled, spend some time comparing and contrasting what the psalmist wants and doesn't want in his life. What is he looking to keep and increase? What does he want to cut out?

Do you see any points of alignment with your life? How might turning these stanzas into a prayer change the way you think and act?

If you've given only a general answer, take some time to ask God if there is something more specific.

OBSERVE the TEXT of SCRIPTURE

READ the Beth stanza and mark every synonym for the Word of God. When you have done that, record below what you learned from this stanza about God's Word.

ב

Beth

9   *How can a young man keep his way pure? By keeping it according to Your word.*

10   *With all my heart I have sought You; do not let me wander from Your commandments.*

11   *Your word I have treasured in my heart, that I may not sin against You.*

12   *Blessed are You, O LORD; teach me Your statutes.*

13   *With my lips I have told of all the ordinances of Your mouth.*

14   *I have rejoiced in the way of Your testimonies, as much as in all riches.*

15   *I will meditate on Your precepts and regard Your ways.*

16   *I shall delight in Your statutes; I shall not forget Your word.*

DISCUSS with your GROUP or PONDER on your own . . .

What did you learn from this stanza about God's Word?

What question does the psalmist open the Beth stanza with?

What kind of relevance does this have in our world today? In your family? In your walk with God?

ONE STEP FURTHER:

Word Study: *choq* / statute
Take some time and investigate the Hebrew word translated "statutes" in verses 12 and 16 of the Beth stanza. Note that the Hebrew words will be slightly different based on suffixes (endings) that account for things like *number* (singular vs. plural), but they trace back to the same root. Remember to do your own research by searching a concordance first and investigating how the word is used in other contexts. After that check out secondary sources such as *Strong's Exhaustive Concordance of the Bible*, the *Theological Wordbook of the Old Testament* (often abbreviated *TWOT*), and *The Complete Word Study Dictionary: Old Testament*.

Does this word carry shades of meaning that distinguish it from *torah* or is it a simple synonym? Record your findings.

Week Two: **Your Source for Answers in a World of Questions**

How does he answer his own question in the text?

FYI:

Wandering . . .

The Hebrew root word used here for wander is *shagah* and primarily indicates a sin that is committed inadvertently, according to the *Theological Wordbook of the Old Testament.* This same Hebrew root is used for straying, as sheep do when they "nibble their way to lost-ness."[2] Like ships they wander, go off course, and so do people.

What do we learn about the psalmist's heart in the Beth stanza?

In each of the heart references, what other focus does the line of text contain? The psalmist has done something with his heart. What and why?

TRUE STORIES:

David's Wandering and Return

If David penned Psalm 119, we have a chilling picture from his own life of how he wandered for a season. In the account, however, we also have the picture of a faithful God who called him back to Himself.

Take some time today to read the account of David from 2 Samuel 11 and 12. Also read Psalm 51 which some think David wrote after his encounter with Bathsheba. Consider what caused David to wander and God's lavish forgiveness, but also the real consequences he reaped.

In verse 10, the psalmist writes, "Do not let me wander from Your commandments." What kind of picture does the word "wander" bring to mind? How has wandering exhibited itself in your life? In the lives of those close to you?

Can you identify anything in your life that cultivates wandering?

What antidotes does the text give to wandering?

Sweeter than Chocolate!®
An Inductive Study of Psalm 119

What does meditating on God's precepts involve? If you're not sure, don't worry, we'll be looking at this more in-depth in future weeks.

Do you have any ideas of how to delight in God's statutes and not forget His words?

The text of Scripture is filled with examples of people who forgot. Why do we so quickly think that we are different? What can we do to guard against falling into the same trap?

ONE STEP FURTHER:

Psalm 119:11 Treasuring His Word

As hard as it may seem to do, memorizing God's Word provides enormous benefits. If you have a little extra time this week, consider browsing through the entire Psalm and picking out several verses or a stanza to memorize. Finding a partner to memorize with you and deciding on a reward in advance may help your resolve.

OBSERVE the TEXT of SCRIPTURE

READ the Gimel stanza and mark every synonym for the Word of God. When you have done that, record below what you learned from this stanza about God's Word.

ג

Gimel

17 *Deal bountifully with Your servant, that I may live and keep Your word.*

18 *Open my eyes, that I may behold wonderful things from Your law.*

19 *I am a stranger in the earth; do not hide Your commandments from me.*

20 *My soul is crushed with longing after Your ordinances at all times.*

21 *You rebuke the arrogant, the cursed, who wander from Your commandments.*

22 *Take away reproach and contempt from me, for I observe Your testimonies.*

23 *Even though princes sit and talk against me, Your servant meditates on Your statutes.*

24 *Your testimonies also are my delight; they are my counselors.*

Sweeter than Chocolate!®
An Inductive Study of Psalm 119

DISCUSS with your GROUP or PONDER on your own . . .

What did you learn from this stanza about God's Word?

FYI:

Sitz im Leben . . .

Oh yeah. Now we're getting scholarly. *Sitz im leben* is German for "setting in life." "What is the life setting of the text?" is a context question. You'll run across this phrase if you read a lot of scholarly journals. Don't let the foreign words throw you off. They are simple words and important to know if you wade into scholarly literature.

How does the tone of this stanza differ from that of Aleph and Beth? What can you glean about the general circumstances of the psalmist's life? What clues from the text suggest this change in tone?

What kinds of people are mentioned in the Gimel stanza? What do you learn about them from the text?

Having just considered the concept of wandering in the Beth stanza, what kind of people wander according to the Gimel stanza?

It is not surprising that given the people the psalmist is dealing with he needs counsel. Consider your own life for a moment. Who was the last person you turned to for counsel? Remember, even if you consulted a book or some form of media, there is a person behind the counsel you received.

Did that person provide you with truth? How do you know?

Who else do you typically turn to for counsel?

We live in an age in which every person looking for a counselor can find countless TV and radio personalities ready to counsel based on any number of different worldviews, to say nothing of friends laden with opinions. What should we make of all the counsel and opinions that swirl around us? Where does the psalmist find his counsel?

How can God's Word be your counselor? Are there conditions in your life that could hinder the effectiveness of God's Word?

Digging Deeper

What else does God's Word say about counselors?

If you can, spend some time this week digging around for what God's Word says about counselors.

Start by considering what you already know about counsel from the Word of God and see if you can show where these truths are in the Bible. Make sure that the Word actually says what you think it says.

Next, run a simple concordance search. See what you can learn from other places in Scripture where the word *counsel* and *counselor* are used.

Do you see main concepts in the texts? If so, what are they?

Finally, consult your word study resources and record pertinent information you did not find on your own.

What have you learned about counsel that you can apply to your life? Can you think of specific applications for the truths you have learned?

If you have questions for future study or other thoughts or applications you want to process on the Gimel passage, jot them down below.

Before moving on to Daleth, spend some quiet time with the Lord praying through the texts that we have been studying and listening in His presence.

OBSERVE the TEXT of SCRIPTURE

READ the Daleth stanza and mark every synonym for the Word of God, then record below what you learned from this stanza about God's Word.

ד

Daleth

25 *My soul cleaves to the dust; revive me according to Your word.*

26 *I have told of my ways, and You have answered me; teach me Your statutes.*

27 *Make me understand the way of Your precepts, so I will meditate on Your wonders.*

28 *My soul weeps because of grief; strengthen me according to Your word.*

29 *Remove the false way from me, and graciously grant me Your law.*

30 *I have chosen the faithful way; I have placed Your ordinances before me.*

31 *I cling to Your testimonies; O LORD, do not put me to shame!*

32 *I shall run the way of Your commandments, for You will enlarge my heart.*

ONE STEP FURTHER:

Word Study: *edah / testimony*

If you have time, investigate the Hebrew word translated "testimonies." Record what you learn and how it compares with the synonyms for God's Word we have looked at so far.

Week Two: **Your Source for Answers in a World of Questions**

DISCUSS with your GROUP or PONDER on your own . . .

What did you learn about the Word of God in the Daleth stanza? Does anything stand out to you as unique from what you have learned so far? If so, what?

ONE STEP FURTHER:

Think on this . . .

What does the New Testament say about trying to live the Christian life on our own power? As you answer, cite references to support your thoughts.

In what general situation does the psalmist finds himself in the Daleth stanza?

What actions does he ask God to take on his behalf? What do all of the actions in some way involve?

ONE STEP FURTHER:

Prayer Survey

If you have some time this week, investigate prayers godly men and women in the Bible have prayed and prayers God answers. Remember to think of synonyms when running concordance searches (pray, ask, request, desire, etc.).

What is the psalmist doing?

How do you see God and the psalmist working together? What outcome do you expect if the psalmist tries to obey on his own power?

Take some time today to consider how praying like the psalmist can impact your walk with God.

Digging Deeper

I Cling to Your Testimonies

What else does God's Word say about *clinging?*

If you can, spend some time this week digging around for what else God's Word says about clinging. Investigate the Hebrew word used. See where else it is used and find out what and who people are supposed to cling to.

FYI:

Enlarge my Heart
Here we see that the psalmist trusts that God will grant him not only a whole heart but also one with increased capacity! May that be one of our continual prayers—that God will give us hearts that are whole toward Him and that are continually growing in their capacity to love and serve Him!

It is interesting that the psalmist uses the same Hebrew word for cleaving to the dust in the beginning of the stanza as he does for clinging to God's testimonies at the end. As human beings, we will cling; the outcome depends on whether we choose wisely and cling to God and His Word.

What things in life do you cling to? Are they pleasing to God? Why/why not?

Week Two: **Your Source for Answers in a World of Questions**

What practical steps can you take to choose God's way and cling to His testimonies today? This week? If you have children, how can you model this to them?

OBSERVE the TEXT of SCRIPTURE

READ the He stanza and mark every synonym for the Word of God. When you have done that, record below what you learned from this stanza about God's Word.

He

33 *Teach me, O LORD, the way of Your statutes, and I shall observe it to the end.*

34 *Give me understanding, that I may observe Your law and keep it with all my heart.*

35 *Make me walk in the path of Your commandments, for I delight in it.*

36 *Incline my heart to Your testimonies and not to dishonest gain.*

37 *Turn away my eyes from looking at vanity, and revive me in Your ways.*

38 *Establish Your word to Your servant, as that which produces reverence for You.*

39 *Turn away my reproach which I dread, for Your ordinances are good.*

40 *Behold, I long for Your precepts; revive me through Your righteousness.*

DISCUSS with your GROUP or PONDER on your own . . .

What did you learn about the Word of God from the He stanza? Are you beginning to see repeated concepts? If so, what? What about new concepts?

Who is the focus of this stanza?

What specifics does the psalmist pray for, both positively and negatively? Which requests can you relate to the most?

It is one thing to observe statutes and keep laws; delighting in commandments, however, is another thing altogether. To what extent do you delight in God's commandments? Explain your response.

FYI:

What is an inclined heart?
It is a heart that is turned towards obedience. Think for a moment of people in your life who have hearts inclined one direction or another. Anyone who has worked with children has probably noticed the difference between children who are inclined to obey and those who are inclined to disobey.

When I think of the inclination of the heart, my mind immediately goes to experiences that I have had on field trips with elementary school children. To protect the not-so-innocent, I'll simply call them Butterfly Boy and Corn Maze Boy. Both students were given specific instructions: "Don't touch the butterflies" and "It's time to leave the corn maze." Neither heart, however, was inclined to obey. One heart was inclined to touch butterflies . . . and did. The other heart was inclined to run back into a corn maze . . . and did. Neither had a heart that was inclined to hear and obey.

What is your heart inclined toward today? To what extent is your heart inclined to hear and obey God's Word?

What kinds of butterflies or corn mazes are you dealing with in your life today?

Digging Deeper

Reverence for God

Set aside some time this week to look at this verse more closely:

> *"Establish Your word to Your servant, as that which produces reverence for You."*

Study the phrase "reverence for You" and see what characterizes a person who has reverence for God and what benefits this brings.

In verse 37, the psalmist prays that God will turn his eyes away from looking at vanity. Vanity is anything that is empty or worthless. Is there anything in your life that while not necessarily "bad" is nonetheless vanity? Why would this even matter to the psalmist? How can turning your eyes from vanity help you align more with God and His Word?

Can you think of a New Testament passage that gives us the antidote for this by telling us what to think about? If not, consider how you can find the answer to this question.

@THE END OF THE DAY . . .

READ Psalm 119:1-40 one last time for the week and summarize the benefits the psalmist claims come from God's Word.

To what extent are these benefits true in your life? To what extent does your life align with Scripture? Why?

What would your life look like if these benefits were fully realized in it? Can you picture your life in this way? Think, again, in terms of specifics.

What would your church look like?

Week Two: **Your Source for Answers in a World of Questions**

What would the world look like?

If possible, spend an hour this week quietly before God considering what you have studied. Take a walk or just sit in a chair and let Him speak to you about His Word that is more and more taking root in your heart.

Week Three
The Secret to Delighting in God

Vav	Zayin	Heth	Teth	Yodh

Looking at the claims of Psalm 119 is just this side of overwhelming. The psalmist casts such a compelling and appealing vision of life with God's Word, a vision of how things could be, of how they should be. Biblically, anyone who chooses to turn away from such a preferred future has to be a fool. And yet for those who have dabbled in the Word, the psalm stirs a strange amalgam of desire and disbelief. After all, how can we account for gaps in our lives—places where our lives do not align with what the Word says should be? What do we make of this? What can we do with this?

The truth of the matter is this: Ever since Adam and Eve sinned in the Garden of Eden mankind has had to deal with the problem of gaps. Jesus came to close the gap in the ultimate sense, but we still deal with gaps in the everydayness of life.

So how do we close the gap between what *is* and what *should be*? What is to be done and who is to do it? How do we come to love and delight in the Word as the psalmist loves and delights in it? Do we work it up on our own or is there another way?

AN OVERVIEW OF THE TEXT

OBSERVE the TEXT of SCRIPTURE

If you have the time, pour a cup of coffee and read through all of Psalm 119. If this doesn't strike you as a delight today, relax and read the Vav through Yodh stanzas (Psalm 119:41-80). Like last week, read with an eye toward asking questions of the text, and when you are done spend some time interacting with the questions that follow.

Vav

41 May Your lovingkindnesses also come to me, O LORD, Your salvation according to Your word;

42 So I will have an answer for him who reproaches me, for I trust in Your word.

43 And do not take the word of truth utterly out of my mouth, for I wait for Your ordinances.

44 So I will keep Your law continually, forever and ever.

45 And I will walk at liberty, for I seek Your precepts.

46 I will also speak of Your testimonies before kings and shall not be ashamed.

47 I shall delight in Your commandments, which I love.

48 And I shall lift up my hands to Your commandments, which I love; and I will meditate on Your statutes.

Zayin

49 Remember the word to Your servant, in which You have made me hope.

50 This is my comfort in my affliction, that Your word has revived me.

51 The arrogant utterly deride me, yet I do not turn aside from Your law.

52 I have remembered Your ordinances from of old, O LORD, and comfort myself.

53 Burning indignation has seized me because of the wicked, who forsake Your law.

54 Your statutes are my songs in the house of my pilgrimage.

55 O LORD, I remember Your name in the night, and keep Your law.

56 This has become mine, that I observe Your precepts.

Heth

57 The LORD is my portion; I have promised to keep Your words.

58 I sought Your favor with all my heart; be gracious to me according to Your word.

59 I considered my ways and turned my feet to Your testimonies.

60 I hastened and did not delay to keep Your commandments.

61 The cords of the wicked have encircled me, but I have not forgotten Your law.

62 At midnight I shall rise to give thanks to You because of Your righteous ordinances.

63 I am a companion of all those who fear You, and of those who keep Your precepts.

64 The earth is full of Your lovingkindness, O LORD; teach me Your statutes.

Teth

65 You have dealt well with Your servant, O LORD, according to Your word.

66 Teach me good discernment and knowledge, for I believe in Your commandments.

67 Before I was afflicted I went astray, but now I keep Your word.

68 You are good and do good; teach me Your statutes.

69 The arrogant have forged a lie against me; with all my heart I will observe Your precepts.

70 Their heart is covered with fat, but I delight in Your law.

71 It is good for me that I was afflicted, that I may learn Your statutes.

72 The law of Your mouth is better to me than thousands of gold and silver pieces.

Week Three: **The Secret to Delighting in God**

Yodh

73 *Your hands made me and fashioned me; give me understanding, that I may learn Your commandments.*

74 *May those who fear You see me and be glad, because I wait for Your word.*

75 *I know, O LORD, that Your judgments are righteous, and that in faithfulness You have afflicted me.*

76 *O may Your lovingkindness comfort me, according to Your word to Your servant.*

77 *May Your compassion come to me that I may live, for Your law is my delight.*

78 *May the arrogant be ashamed, for they subvert me with a lie; but I shall meditate on Your precepts.*

79 *May those who fear You turn to me, even those who know Your testimonies.*

80 *May my heart be blameless in Your statutes, so that I will not be ashamed.*

DISCUSS with your GROUP or PONDER on your own . . .

What are your initial observations on the text?

What questions surface in your mind?

What words or phrases might you focus on for further study?

What has been your biggest application point so far? If you have several, take some time to consider which has been the most important and then see if there are concepts in the text this week that are related and record them below.

OBSERVE the TEXT of SCRIPTURE

READ Vav through Yodh (Psalm 119:41-80) again and consider the ways in which the psalmist is working with God.

In the first five stanzas (Aleph, Beth, Gimel, Daleth, and He), we considered what the psalmist asked God to do in his life, what he prayed for and against. In the Vav through Yodh stanzas, we're going to consider some of the ways the psalmist is working with God.

Week Three: **The Secret to Delighting in God**

In the space below, make a simple list of everything the psalmist says he is doing or will do. We'll call this our "man" list, as it is the human side of the relationship, what the psalmist is investing.

Read Vav through Yodh again and make a "God" list. Include the benefits that the psalmist has seen either through what God has done or what the psalmist trusts He will do. Include anything you learn about God and His nature.

When you consider the lists side by side, what thoughts come to your mind regarding the relationship between what God does and what the psalmist does? What concepts do you see that you can apply in your life?

OBSERVE the TEXT of SCRIPTURE

READ the Vav stanza and mark every synonym for the Word of God. Record below what you learned about God's Word from this stanza.

ו

Vav

41 *May Your lovingkindnesses also come to me, O LORD, Your salvation according to Your word;*

42 *So I will have an answer for him who reproaches me, for I trust in Your word.*

43 *And do not take the word of truth utterly out of my mouth, for I wait for Your ordinances.*

44 *So I will keep Your law continually, forever and ever.*

45 *And I will walk at liberty, for I seek Your precepts.*

46 *I will also speak of Your testimonies before kings and shall not be ashamed.*

47 *I shall delight in Your commandments, which I love.*

48 *And I shall lift up my hands to Your commandments, which I love; and I will meditate on Your statutes.*

DISCUSS with your GROUP or PONDER on your own . . .

What did you learn from this stanza about God's Word?

What does this stanza suggest about the psalmist's life situation? What type of people are crossing his path and how does he interact with them?

ONE STEP FURTHER:

Continually . . .
If you have time, look into the word in verse 44 translated "continually." Note the contexts in which it is often used.

FYI:

Unplumbable depths . . .
As I'm writing, the volume of opportunity for study has been blowing me away. In six weeks, there are only so many rocks you can overturn, there are only so many word studies you can complete, and there are only so many concepts that you can learn and absorb. That said, however, instead of lamenting that we cannot plumb the depths of this passage, I am learning to rejoice *in the fact that we cannot plumb the depths of this passage.* No matter how much we study, no matter how much we meditate and apply, God's Word remains full and overflowing for us to come back and draw out even more. I think I am like the psalmist who both *has* God's Word and *waits for* God's Word. When there seems to be too much don't fret; instead REJOICE in God's lavish abundance!

When people reproach you, how do you answer? Do you respond as a person who trusts in the Word? Do people notice that the ways you respond are different from the ways others around you respond? Explain.

FYI:

Rahab

In verse 45, the word that is translated as "liberty" is the Hebrew word *rahab* which generally carries the meaning of wide, broad, or spacious. Yes, it is the same word as *that* Rahab.

In verses 45 through 48, we see some very uncommon pairings of words. How does the psalmist describe his views about God's commandments and precepts in these verses?

FYI:

An officer in the rearview mirror . . .

Driving home from my daughter's softball game recently, I found myself being followed by one of Gurnee's finest. I wasn't speeding (at the moment) and my registration was current. Everything was in order except that I had forgotten my purse at home. Hence, I was driving without my license and proof of insurance. Details, yes, but significant ones if I would happen to be pulled over. I was not in compliance with the law, and thus, I was not driving at ease.

The Jewish Publication Society translates Psalm 119:45, "I will walk about at ease, for I have turned to Your precepts." Even if I had my license, I'm not sure that I would have been driving "at ease" with the Law in my rearview mirror. If, however, the officer in the car behind me was my father or a close friend, someone I had a relationship with, my outlook would have been different. Relationship makes all the difference in the world.[3]

How is your outlook similar to or different than that of the psalmist? How does this show up in your behavior?

Can you honestly say with the psalmist, "Lord, I love your commandments!"? What is the greatest love of your life? How does God's Word rank in comparison?

Since there seems to be an intimate connection between delighting in and keeping God's Word, the significant question to ask is this: *Where does this delight come from and how can I get it?*

To answer this question, spend some time considering biblical characters who delighted in God and begin compiling a list of those you want to investigate.

The psalmist who penned Psalm 119 is certainly worthy of consideration. While we cannot say definitively that it was David, we know that David loved God with his whole heart. We are also told that David was a man after God's own heart. Because of these things, David's faith is a great place to start sniffing around for clues on how to delight in God.

Although you may want to pursue some other avenues, as we focus in on David for the moment, where are some places we can look to find his best days with God? If you're not sure, how can you find out?

QUIZ:

Write your Letters
Without looking, try writing the names of the first ten stanzas of Psalm 119 along with the corresponding Hebrew letters.

1.

2.

3.

4.

5.

6.

7.

8.

9.

10.

Digging Deeper

Where do I get the delight?

While we will learn much about David in 1 and 2 Samuel and in the Psalms generally, one place we can focus on is Psalm 27. **READ** Psalm 27 and record what David asks God for. We often talk about Solomon's request, but David's is the more life-altering of the two.

What does God tell David to do?

Describe David's relationship with God. Is it strictly legal or something more?

Can you think of New Testament references to the concepts of dwelling, abiding, and seeking? Explain.

Spend some time today in John 15 and consider what Jesus says about abiding and asking.

If you have not been delighting in God's Word, if it has not been the love of your life, based on what you read today, how can you make it your life's passion?

A thought for the day:

Living the Word comes out of loving the Word!

OBSERVE the TEXT of SCRIPTURE

READ the Zayin stanza and mark every synonym for the Word of God. Record below what you learned about God's Word from this stanza.

ז

Zayin

49 *Remember the word to Your servant, in which You have made me hope.*

50 *This is my comfort in my affliction, that Your word has revived me.*

51 *The arrogant utterly deride me, yet I do not turn aside from Your law.*

52 *I have remembered Your ordinances from of old, O LORD, and comfort myself.*

53 *Burning indignation has seized me because of the wicked, who forsake Your law.*

54 *Your statutes are my songs in the house of my pilgrimage.*

55 *O LORD, I remember Your name in the night, and keep Your law.*

56 *This has become mine, that I observe Your precepts.*

DISCUSS with your GROUP or PONDER on your own . . .

What did you learn from this stanza about God's Word?

Notes

FYI:

David Justified by Faith

Although David lived under the Law, he sought to dwell in God's presence, to seek and be in relationship with the Lawgiver. Listen to how Paul puts it in the book of Romans 4:5-8, "But to the one who does not work, but believes in Him who justifies the ungodly, his faith is credited as righteousness, just as David also speaks of the blessing on the man to whom God credits righteousness apart from works: "BLESSED ARE THOSE WHOSE LAWLESS DEEDS HAVE BEEN FORGIVEN, AND WHOSE SINS HAVE BEEN COVERED. BLESSED IS THE MAN WHOSE SIN THE LORD WILL NOT TAKE INTO ACCOUNT."

TRUE STORIES:

Moses and Joshua

These two men also followed God with whole hearts. If you have time this week, read Exodus 33 and consider some of the ways their pursuit of God is demonstrated in the text.

FYI:

Something to watch . . .

In verse 53 the psalmist talks about the "burning indignation" he has over the wicked. Keep an eye on how his views toward the lawless progress.

Sweeter than Chocolate!®
An Inductive Study of Psalm 119

Week Three: **The Secret to Delighting in God**

In what kind of circumstances does the psalmist find himself in this stanza?

How are the people he refers to treating him?

How does he respond to his situation? Under similar circumstances how would you respond or react? Why?

The psalmist talks about comforting himself by remembering God's ordinances of old. How can you comfort yourself using God's Word? If you're thinking generally, shift gears and write down some specifics. Consider a situation in your life where you need comfort and apply God's specific Word to your specific need. If you're finding this tough, don't worry. Pray some more and if you need to, call a wise friend to help guide you through it.

The psalmist uses the word "remember" three times in this stanza. Why was remembering important to him? What purpose did it serve?

How are you at remembering? What causes you to remember or to forget? Are there any steps you can take to be more purposeful in remembering?

How will your life change if you begin to remember *purposefully*?

Finally, how adept are you at comforting yourself from God's Word?

What keeps you from comforting yourself from God's Word? How can you improve in this area?

ONE STEP FURTHER:

Word Study: Remember

Take some time and investigate what God says about remembering. Who is supposed to remember, what, and about whom? Find the Hebrew word used in this stanza and go from there. Record pertinent findings below.

ONE STEP FURTHER

The God of all comfort . . .

If you can, spend some time reading this week in 2 Corinthians about the God of all comfort. Record your biggest application point in the space below.

Sweeter than Chocolate!®

Week Three: **The Secret to Delighting in God**

OBSERVE the TEXT of SCRIPTURE

READ the Heth stanza and mark every synonym for the Word of God. Record below what you learned about God's Word from this stanza.

ח

Heth

57 *The LORD is my portion; I have promised to keep Your words.*

58 *I sought Your favor with all my heart; be gracious to me according to Your word.*

59 *I considered my ways and turned my feet to Your testimonies.*

60 *I hastened and did not delay to keep Your commandments.*

61 *The cords of the wicked have encircled me, but I have not forgotten Your law.*

62 *At midnight I shall rise to give thanks to You because of Your righteous ordinances.*

63 *I am a companion of all those who fear You, and of those who keep Your precepts.*

64 *The earth is full of Your lovingkindness, O LORD; teach me Your statutes.*

DISCUSS with your GROUP or PONDER on your own . . .

What did you learn from this stanza about God's Word?

Look closely at verses 57 through 60 and summarize what the psalmist wants and what actions he has taken.

How would considering your ways benefit you? Have you done this recently? Have you ever done this? If it's been some time, why don't you put your pencil down right now and go take a quiet walk with God, be quiet before Him, and consider your ways.

How does your life align with God's ways? Is there any work that God and you need to do? Explain.

What does turning your feet to God's testimonies mean?

Are you quick to obey God and to follow the promptings of His Spirit? If not, ask God to help you obey and *remember* the example of the Israelites' delayed obedience.

ONE STEP FURTHER:

Word Study: Portion

If you have some time this week, check out the Hebrew word for "portion." How was the word typically used? What was usually portioned and who got what? Record interesting facts below.

TRUE STORIES:

Delayed obedience is disobedience . . .

In life certain phrases just stick with you. I first heard "Delayed obedience is disobedience" at a youth conference called SEMP (Student Evangelism Mission Project) during the 1990s. Not sure if you buy it? Read the account of Israel's first attempt to enter the promised land and then we'll talk. You'll find it in Numbers 13 and 14.

Week Three: **The Secret to Delighting in God**

Digging Deeper

Belief and Obedience

Can true belief live from the neck up? Is belief something that happens just in the brain or does it involve the whole life? In the text before us today we see that the psalmist knew the Word, considered his ways, and then turned his feet to God's ways without delay. Was he just a really good guy or is this the normal pattern of authentic belief? Does belief involve obedience? Can you think of places where God's Word addresses this question? If you're not sure, what words or phrases might yield a productive concordance search to get you started?

Let's take a little time together to look at the children of Israel's first attempt at entering the promised land. We'll look at the event first in the Old Testament and then we'll examine the commentary the author of the New Testament book of Hebrews provides.

READ Numbers 13 and 14. Summarize the situation and note the outcome.

Now **READ** Hebrews 3. According to verse 19, why were the people not able to enter the promised land? What synonym is used in verse 18? Explain how the two concepts tie together.

Finally, **READ** John 3 noting what the evangelist says about both belief and obedience.

Based on the texts we have looked at, plus any you have researched on your own, how do belief and obedience relate?

In verse 63, the psalmist says "I am a companion of all those who fear You . . . ." If this is David, who are these people and what kind of effect did they have on his life?

Do you have companions in your life who fear God? What influences do they have on you? How do you influence them?

ONE STEP FURTHER:

Righteous Companions

If you have some extra time this week, consider what God's Word says about how the company we keep impacts our lives. The book of Proverbs particularly will give you much insight into this topic. As one friend of mine says, "You become what you hang out with!" Record what you learn below.

TRUE STORIES:

David and his Companions

If David penned 119, his companions included Samuel and Jonathan. Spend some time this week reading and considering their stories in 1 Samuel 18–23. There's bonus material in there, so it's well worthwhile!

Sweeter than Chocolate!®

An Inductive Study of Psalm 119

Week Three: **The Secret to Delighting in God**

OBSERVE the TEXT of SCRIPTURE

READ the Teth stanza and mark every synonym for the Word of God. Record below what you learned about God's Word from this stanza.

Teth

65 *You have dealt well with Your servant, O LORD, according to Your word.*

66 *Teach me good discernment and knowledge, for I believe in Your commandments.*

67 *Before I was afflicted I went astray, but now I keep Your word.*

68 *You are good and do good; teach me Your statutes.*

69 *The arrogant have forged a lie against me; with all my heart I will observe Your precepts.*

70 *Their heart is covered with fat, but I delight in Your law.*

71 *It is good for me that I was afflicted, that I may learn Your statutes.*

72 *The law of Your mouth is better to me than thousands of gold and silver pieces.*

DISCUSS with your GROUP or PONDER on your own . . .

What did you learn from this stanza about God's Word?

What general event does the psalmist refer to that changed the way he lived?

How does the psalmist view affliction? How does this square with the way our culture thinks?

How does our culture typically respond to God in the midst of affliction? How does this compare with the psalmist's response?

Do you respond to affliction more like our culture or the psalmist? Explain.

What is the psalmist's view of God? When you respond, quote directly from the text of Scripture . . . and memorize the answer!

How can he know this?

Notes

Do you know for sure that God is good and does good? Does anything ever cause you to question this? If so, how can you resolve this question for yourself?

FYI:

Thoughts about God

What comes into your mind when you think about God? According to A.W. Tozer, author of *The Knowledge of the Holy*, there is nothing that is more important.[4] Our thoughts about God affect everything else. We need to make sure that these thoughts are based on His Word and not our imaginations.

How do you respond when the storms of life hit?

Consider some times in your life when you encountered affliction. Do you always respond in similar fashions? If you have responded differently, compare and contrast times when you responded biblically and not so biblically.

Did you learn from one kind of response or both? If so, what?

Digging Deeper

Knowing God

We could dig in so many different places in this stanza. We could talk about discernment, we could look more into affliction or talk about being the victim of lies, but there is nothing more important in this stanza, or in the Bible for that matter, than the character of God. In the midst of affliction, the psalmist confidently proclaims, "You are good and do good."

When you're afflicted, where do you go in God's Word for bedrock truths about God? Where does God talk about Himself? Where does He describe who He is and what does He say about Himself? If you're scratching your head, here are a few passages to investigate that the psalmist would certainly have known and loved: Genesis 17:1-8; Exodus 3; Exodus 34:6-7; Deuteronomy 6.

Then the LORD passed by in front of him and proclaimed,

"The LORD, the LORD God, compassionate and gracious, slow to anger, and abounding in lovingkindness and truth; who keeps lovingkindness for thousands, who forgives iniquity, transgression and sin; yet He will by no means leave the guilty unpunished, visiting the iniquity of fathers on the children and on the grandchildren to the third and fourth generations."

Exodus 34:6-7

If you can, set aside at least an hour to be quiet and consider your view of God. Ask God to show you where your views can be more aligned with His truth.

God is good and does good!

BEDROCK TRUTHS:

God is Good and Does Good
There are truths and then there are TRUTHS. This is bedrock truth. This truth about God is so foundational that if this were the only truth you grasped and took away from this study, it would be enough. *God is good and does good.*

OBSERVE the TEXT of SCRIPTURE

READ the Yodh stanza and mark every synonym for the Word of God. Record below what you learned about God's Word from this stanza.

ʼ

Yodh

73 *Your hands made me and fashioned me; give me understanding, that I may learn Your commandments.*

74 *May those who fear You see me and be glad, because I wait for Your word.*

75 *I know, O LORD, that Your judgments are righteous, and that in faithfulness You have afflicted me.*

76 *O may Your lovingkindness comfort me, according to Your word to Your servant.*

77 *May Your compassion come to me that I may live, for Your law is my delight.*

78 *May the arrogant be ashamed, for they subvert me with a lie; but I shall meditate on Your precepts.*

79 *May those who fear You turn to me, even those who know Your testimonies.*

80 *May my heart be blameless in Your statutes, so that I will not be ashamed.*

DISCUSS with your GROUP or PONDER on your own . . .

What did you learn from this stanza about God's Word?

What actions does the psalmist attribute to God in the first three verses of the stanza?

What does the psalmist ask for in this stanza? Does he think God will answer him? Why/why not?

Does the psalmist's no-nonsense view on affliction surprise you? Is it simplistic or does it make sense considering the context of the Psalm so far? Explain.

Look closely at verse 77. Although the psalmist delights in God's law, meditates on it, and seeks to keep it, what is it that causes him to live? Is it his law-keeping or something else? Explain.

Read the Yodh stanza again and consider what the psalmist thinks is worse than being afflicted. How does affliction relate to this worse situation?

Do people in our culture prefer to be afflicted or ashamed? How does this reflect the state of our souls? What does it say about our view of God?

ONE STEP FURTHER:

Word Study: Afflicted
Take some time to investigate the Hebrew word translated "afflicted." If the psalmist has been afflicted, what negative in the stanza does this counteract? Record your findings below.

Digging Deeper

The Peaceful Fruit of Righteousness

As we draw near the end of our study this week, spend some time reading Hebrews 12:1-17 and considering how God's discipline parallels the concept of affliction in the Psalms. You've worked hard this week, so don't overdo this assignment. Simply read the text prayerfully and record your thoughts below.

@THE END OF THE DAY . . .

In the Vav, Zayin, Heth, Teth, and Yodh stanzas the psalmist turns the jewel of Scripture to show us his delight in and love for God's Word, which brings liberty and comfort, calls for obedience, and shows forth the goodness and compassion of God.

What facet of this jewel has shone most brightly in your life this week? Is there an area of your life God is calling you to turn your feet from to His testimonies, to hasten and not delay? Consider this question before Him in prayer as we bring this week's lesson to a close and record thoughts He brings to your mind in the space below.

Remember, God is good and does good!

Week Four

Are You Standing Firm in an Unsteady Culture?

 כ   ל   מ   נ

Kaph   Lamedh   Mem   Nun

Although affliction and persecution follow the psalmist, his tenacious hold on the Word of God produces staggering results. Not only does the Word he so loves bring comfort and revival to his soul during the course of his trials, it also brings unparalleled wisdom that can only be attributed to a divine Instructor. The Word lights his path and is the love of his life and the joy of his heart. Can we get the same monumental results the psalmist did? Can you imagine what life will look like when the Word is truly sweeter than chocolate to us? Imagine what our lives will look like when His law is our meditation all day. Let's consider these possibilities as we open our study today!

AN OVERVIEW OF THE TEXT

OBSERVE the TEXT of SCRIPTURE

As we begin today, take time to read through the text we have studied so far and consider the ways God's Word has been working during your time in this Psalm.

READ Psalm 119:81-112, the Kaph, Lamedh, Mem and Nun stanzas, again making initial observations of the text and beginning to identify questions you think we may want to pursue. Remember, exegesis is all about asking questions and there is no such thing as a dumb question. Soon you'll find that asking questions as you read (interacting with the text) is second nature to you. Like everything else though, it will take a little time.

Kaph

81 *My soul languishes for Your salvation; I wait for Your word.*

82 *My eyes fail with longing for Your word, while I say, "When will You comfort me?"*

83 *Though I have become like a wineskin in the smoke, I do not forget Your statutes.*

84 *How many are the days of Your servant? When will You execute judgment on those who persecute me?*

85 *The arrogant have dug pits for me, men who are not in accord with Your law.*

86 *All Your commandments are faithful; they have persecuted me with a lie; help me!*

87 *They almost destroyed me on earth, but as for me, I did not forsake Your precepts.*

88 *Revive me according to Your lovingkindness, so that I may keep the testimony of Your mouth.*

QUIZ:

Name the First Ten Stanzas
(Open book if you need it!)

Without looking, try writing the names of the first ten stanzas of Psalm 119 with the corresponding Hebrew letters.

1.

2.

3.

4.

5.

6.

7.

8.

9.

10.

Lamedh

89 *Forever, O LORD, Your word is settled in heaven.*

90 *Your faithfulness continues throughout all generations; You established the earth,
and it stands.*

91 *They stand this day according to Your ordinances, for all things are Your servants.*

92 *If Your law had not been my delight, then I would have perished in my affliction.*

93 *I will never forget Your precepts, for by them You have revived me.*

94 *I am Yours, save me; for I have sought Your precepts.*

95 *The wicked wait for me to destroy me; I shall diligently consider Your testimonies.*

96 *I have seen a limit to all perfection; Your commandment is exceedingly broad.*

מ
Mem

97   O how I love Your law! It is my meditation all the day.

98   Your commandments make me wiser than my enemies, for they are ever mine.

99   I have more insight than all my teachers, for Your testimonies are my meditation.

100   I understand more than the aged, because I have observed Your precepts.

101   I have restrained my feet from every evil way, that I may keep Your word.

102   I have not turned aside from Your ordinances, for You Yourself have taught me.

103   How sweet are Your words to my taste! Yes, sweeter *than* honey to my mouth!

104   From Your precepts I get understanding; therefore I hate every false way.

נ
Nun

105   Your word is a lamp to my feet and a light to my path.

106   I have sworn and I will confirm it, that I will keep Your righteous ordinances.

107   I am exceedingly afflicted; revive me, O LORD, according to Your word.

108   O accept the freewill offerings of my mouth, O LORD, and teach me Your ordinances.

109   My life is continually in my hand, yet I do not forget Your law.

110   The wicked have laid a snare for me, yet I have not gone astray from Your precepts.

111   I have inherited Your testimonies forever, for they are the joy of my heart.

112   I have inclined my heart to perform Your statutes forever, even *to* the end.

DISCUSS with your GROUP or PONDER on your own . . .

What are your initial observations on the text?

ONE STEP FURTHER:

The Hebrew Alphabet

If you're learning the Hebrew alphabet, take a few minutes and write the next four letters below. Write each letter 10 times on a line and say the name aloud. Don't forget to keep practicing the letters you've already learned!

1.

2.

3.

4.

What questions surface in your mind?

What words and phrases can you focus on for further study?

Has your thinking changed since you have been studying this Psalm? What about your behavior? Are there areas God is convicting you of, but you're resisting? If so, take a few minutes and jot those areas down. If you're not comfortable putting them here, write them down on a separate piece of paper; just get them in front of your eyes and out of the recesses of your brain. Also see if you can identify why you are disobeying. Is it fear? Pride? Something else? Sometimes looking at an issue in black and white helps us obey.

OBSERVE the TEXT of SCRIPTURE

READ Kaph through Nun (Psalm 119:81-112) again. This time compile two simple lists. In one, record the objective benefits of the Word. In the other, list the subjective feelings the psalmist has about the Word. Here are a couple to get you started.

OBJECTIVE	SUBJECTIVE
v. 86	v. 92
All Your commandments are faithful	The law is the psalmist's delight

Looking over the lists you've compiled, have you experienced the subjective feelings of the psalmist? Are you beginning to view the Word as sweeter than chocolate or would you honestly rather have a Dove bar? Explain.

ONE STEP FURTHER:

"I do believe; help my unbelief."

Mark, the writer of the second gospel account, captures the heart of the struggle between belief and unbelief in a pericope about a father and his demon-possessed son. This passage provides balm for the souls of those who find themselves fighting to believe. You can read the story in Mark 9:14-29.

If you resonate with the psalmist there is a very high likelihood you believe the objective claims he makes as well. If you can't relate to the feelings, take some time to closely look at the objective claims and see if there is any area in which you are struggling to take God at His Word. Don't blast by this too quickly. Ever since the Garden, the adversary has been whispering in our ears, "Has God said?" and many of us let that infected sliver of doubt slide in more often than we'd like to admit. But if we're aware of his tactics we're more able to stand firm. So if you have a hard time with any of the objective statements, write them down and make them a matter of prayer between you and God. (e.g. Do I believe His Word can revive me? Do I believe His Word is settled in the heavens?, etc.)

FYI:

So what's a pericope?

Pericope (pronounced per-ik'-o-pee) simply means "a selection from a book," according to Merriam-Webster.[5] Theologians use the word to talk about sections of Scripture. Often you'll find pericopes in your Bible separated by headings over portions of text within a chapter. Why do you need to know this word? You don't, but if you start reading scholarly commentaries it is a piece of jargon that you will eventually run into.

If you need to do any alignment business with God, take some time for that now. Write a prayer or go for a walk and talk it over with Him. Either way, take some time to be quiet in His presence.

OBSERVE the TEXT of SCRIPTURE

READ the Kaph stanza and mark every synonym for the Word of God. When you have done that, record below what you learned from this stanza about God's Word.

Kaph

81 *My soul languishes for Your salvation; I wait for Your word.*

82 *My eyes fail with longing for Your word, while I say, "When will You comfort me?"*

83 *Though I have become like a wineskin in the smoke, I do not forget Your statutes.*

84 *How many are the days of Your servant? When will You execute judgment on those who persecute me?*

85 *The arrogant have dug pits for me, men who are not in accord with Your law.*

86 *All Your commandments are faithful; they have persecuted me with a lie; help me!*

87 *They almost destroyed me on earth, but as for me, I did not forsake Your precepts.*

88 *Revive me according to Your lovingkindness, so that I may keep the testimony of Your mouth.*

DISCUSS with your GROUP or PONDER on your own . . .

What did you learn from this stanza about God's Word?

ONE STEP FURTHER:

Questioning God

The psalmist asks God several questions in this stanza. Here's one to take some time with: *Is it right to question God?* What examples do we have in Scripture? What can we learn from them?

CONSIDER THIS:

Forgetting and Forsaking

When times get tough, two major temptations are either to forget or forsake God and His ways. The psalmist does neither. Do you react one of these ways when life is heading south? Paying attention to how we typically respond to negative situations can help us know where to go in God's Word to fight our fleshy impulses and reactions. My tendency to worry falls under the category of "forgetting God." Because I know that about myself, I spend a lot of time meditating on passages like Matthew 6.

Sweeter than Chocolate!®

An Inductive Study of Psalm 119

What is the psalmist's situation in the Kaph stanza? What is he experiencing?

How does the psalmist respond and/or react? Explain.

What questions does the psalmist ask God?

Do you relate with the psalmist's frame of mind in this stanza? Explain.

We see that the psalmist is being persecuted by a lie. How do you respond differently to persecutions based on truths or lies? Explain your answer.

FYI:

Standing Firm in the Sand of Culture
With our culture's relativistic immorality, it's increasingly important for people to know truth. We can only do this by remembering God's statutes and refusing to forsake His precepts.

Have you ever been persecuted with a lie? How did you handle it?

What can you do when a lie is prevailing against you? Can you think of examples from Scripture or instructions when we are faced with this type of situation? Explain.

Week Four: **Are You Standing Firm in an Unsteady Culture?**

What actions does the psalmist take in his dire situation?

ONE STEP FURTHER:

Word Study: Languishes

If you have some additional time, do some digging on the word translated "languishes" in verse 81. Record what you learn and note the other two words in the stanza from the same Hebrew root.

What have you learned from the Kaph stanza that you can apply to your own life situation? If you're thinking in generalities, try to narrow your focus to a specific situation and response.

Digging Deeper

From the Pit to the Palace

The psalmist who so loved the Torah undoubtedly resonated with Joseph, a young man who was thrown into a pit and persecuted with lies but who God eventually delivered in a miraculous way.

Let's take some time today and examine the life of this man who faced immense trials and came out on top (okay, second to the top).

READ the account of Joseph in Genesis 37 and 39–41. For the whole story, read through chapter 50. As you read, answer the following questions:

How many people came against Joseph? Who were they and how did they come against him?

What authority did those who came against Joseph hold?

How many times was Joseph saved from death? (**READ** the story of Potiphar's wife carefully. Consider what would normally happen to a slave who attempted to rape his master's wife.) Explain.

What types of deception and/or evil practices were used against Joseph? How did he respond to the continued injustice?

FYI:

Jeremiah Facts

Name:	Jeremiah
Occupation:	Prophet
Target Audience:	Judah (the Southern Kingdom)
Nickname:	The Weeping Prophet
Interesting Fact:	Jeremiah prophesied about the fall of Jerusalem in 586 BC and lived to witness it.

Sweeter than Chocolate!®

An Inductive Study of Psalm 119

Week Four: **Are You Standing Firm in an Unsteady Culture?**

What was God doing in all of this? If you have read through chapter 50, what did Joseph say?

What have you learned about God from this account?

List some practical applications from the account of Joseph you can apply in your life today.

OBSERVE the TEXT of SCRIPTURE

READ the Lamedh stanza and mark every synonym for the Word of God. When you have done that, record below what you learned from this stanza about God's Word.

Lamedh

89 *Forever, O LORD, Your word is settled in heaven.*

90 *Your faithfulness continues throughout all generations; You established the earth,*
   and it stands.

91 *They stand this day according to Your ordinances, for all things are Your servants.*

92 *If Your law had not been my delight, then I would have perished in my affliction.*

93 *I will never forget Your precepts, for by them You have revived me.*

94 *I am Yours, save me; for I have sought Your precepts.*

95 *The wicked wait for me to destroy me; I shall diligently consider Your testimonies.*

96 *I have seen a limit to all perfection; Your commandment is exceedingly broad.*

DISCUSS with your GROUP or PONDER on your own . . .

What did you learn from this stanza about God's Word?

Week Four: **Are You Standing Firm in an Unsteady Culture?**

How does the Lamedh stanza differ in tone and scope from the Kaph stanza? Do you sense more hope? Why?

In Kaph we saw ephemeral persecution, trials that in the scope of eternity are gone like a vapor. In the Lamedh stanza we see words of stability and duration. Read through verses 89-91 and make two simple lists. In the first, record words that imply stability. In the second, take note of words that have to do with duration.

Stability   **Duration**

As time permits, investigate some of the words you listed in the Stability column.

Summarize below what you learned about the stability and duration of God and His Word.

How can you apply these truths during times of trial?

Think of some ways your thoughts and actions would change if you lived in the light of the fact that God's Word is "settled in heaven."

CONSIDER THIS:

Nothing settled . . .

In American culture, nothing is settled. Every word, every action, is parsed and reinterpreted. Given this influence, it's increasingly difficult to stand up for "settled" truth. Right thinking is a discipline that is becoming more and more essential as morality in our culture erodes.

Did you notice requests in Kaph that are answered in Lamedh? If so cite them.

FYI:

Isaiah 59:14-15a

"Justice is turned back,
And righteousness stands far away;
For truth has stumbled in the street,
And uprightness cannot enter.
Yes, truth is lacking;
And he who turns aside from evil makes himself a prey."

Spend some time reading through the Lamedh stanza again, this time focusing on God. According to the psalmist, what "belongs" to God? (Yes, I know everything does, but humor me and look closely at the psalmist's take.) In speaking to the LORD, what does the he say is "Yours"? Record what you find below.

Don't you love the fact that within a universe created by God, that belongs to God, the psalmist declares in intimate terms, "I am Yours"? He is not only the God of this universe, He is also the psalmist's God. He is your God and He is my God!

Digging Deeper

Looking at Different Translations

One study method you may already be using is looking at several translations of the same verse. Let's see how this sheds additional light on the last verse of the Lamedh stanza, Psalm 119:96:

> "I have seen a limit to all perfection; Your commandment is exceedingly broad."

This statement may be entirely clear to some. To others of us, though, it leaves perplexed looks on our faces. The phrase "a limit to all perfection" isn't clear to me. Given that, let's take a look at a few other renderings of this particular verse with the help of Logos Bible Software (www.logos.com):[7]

I have seen an end of all perfection: thy commandment is exceeding broad. — DARBY

I have seen an end of all perfection; But thy commandment is exceeding broad. —ASV

I have seen an end of all perfection: But thy commandment is exceeding broad. —AV 1873

I have seen a limit to all perfection, but your commandment is exceedingly broad. —ESV

I have learnt that everything has limits; but your commandment is perfect. —GNT

I have seen a limit to all perfection, but Your command is without limit. —HCSB

Sweeter than Chocolate!®
An Inductive Study of Psalm 119

ONE STEP FURTHER:

"I am Yours" . . .
Another Psalm that embodies the "I am Yours" truth is Psalm 91. Spend some time meditating on this Psalm throughout the week. Then pick a favorite verse or two from the Psalm and commit it to memory. Here's one possibility:

> He will cover you with His pinions,
> And under His wings you may seek refuge;
> His faithfulness is a shield and bulwark.
> –Psalm 91:4

ONE STEP FURTHER:

The God who established the earth . . .
Spend some time considering the person and character of God. Where in Scripture do we have extended passages that tell us about His greatness? How can you locate them on your own?

One such passage is Isaiah 40. Prayerfully read through this scripture and consider its implications.

I have seen an end of all perfection: but thy commandment is exceeding broad.
    —KJV

I see the limits to everything human, but the horizons can't contain your
    commands!
    —The Message

I realize that everything has its limits, but your commands are beyond full
    comprehension.—NET

I have seen the limits of all perfection, but your command is without bounds.—
    NABWRNT

I have seen a limit to all perfection; Your commandment is exceedingly broad.
    —NASB95

Everything I see has its limits, but your commands have none.—NCV

I've learned that everything has its limits. But your commands are perfect.
    They are always there when I need them. —NirV

To all perfection I see a limit; but your commands are boundless. —NIV

I have seen the consummation of all perfection, But Your commandment is
    exceedingly broad. —NKJV

Even perfection has its limits, but your commands have no limit.—NLT

I have seen a limit to all perfection, but your commandment is exceedingly
    broad. —NRSV

I have seen a limit to all perfection, but thy commandment is exceedingly
    broad.—RSV

To all perfection I see a limit, but your commands are boundless.—TNIV

Now that you've looked at these other translations, do you see some common threads of meaning?

Is comparison the perfect way to zero in on the best translation? No. Reading different translators' work, though, gives additional perspective on the text at hand. It is another tool.

Notes

Week Four: **Are You Standing Firm in an Unsteady Culture?**

What single concept from the Lamedh stanza was most impressed on your heart? How can you apply it to your life today? This week?

Record below other thoughts and questions you have on the Lamedh stanza.

OBSERVE the TEXT of SCRIPTURE

READ the Mem stanza and mark every synonym for the Word of God. When you have done that, record below what you learned from this stanza about God's Word.

Mem

97 O how I love Your law! It is my meditation all the day.

98 Your commandments make me wiser than my enemies, for they are ever mine.

99 I have more insight than all my teachers, for Your testimonies are my meditation.

100 I understand more than the aged, because I have observed Your precepts.

101 I have restrained my feet from every evil way, that I may keep Your word.

102 I have not turned aside from Your ordinances, for You Yourself have taught me.

103 How sweet are Your words to my taste! Yes, sweeter than honey to my mouth!

104 From Your precepts I get understanding; therefore I hate every false way.

DISCUSS with your GROUP or PONDER on your own . . .

What did you learn about the Word of God from the Mem stanza? Does anything stand out to you as unique from what you have learned so far? If so, what?

Do you notice anything about the Mem stanza distinct from what we have studied so far? (Perhaps in what it does *not* contain?)

ONE STEP FURTHER:

Word Study:
piqqud / precept

If you have some extra time this week, see what you can find out about the Hebrew word translated "precepts."

What is the theme of the Mem stanza? Watch for the shift in focus between the first and second halves.

Take a few minutes to consider the benefits the psalmist says come from the Word, as well as the actions he has taken. If it helps, you can make a simple list in the margin to identify these. Then record your thoughts on how the benefits and actions relate.

Consider your life for a moment. Does what you know about the Word of God translate into action? Do your hands and feet do what your brain knows is right or have you experienced something of a spiritual paralysis? Explain.

Digging Deeper

A Cure for Spiritual Paralysis: Meditation

While meditation carries something of a mystical eastern religion stigma in the minds of many people, the concept appears throughout the Bible. It is not an emptying of the mind, nor is it only for the spiritual "elite." In fact, if you're a worrier, it's already something you're an expert at in the negative sense. So this week, take some time to see what God's Word says on this topic. Search on the word that appears in Psalm 119 plus other words translated "meditate" in the Bible. Note how they are used.

Look closely at the first chapter of Joshua in your study.

Record your questions, observations, and applications in the space below.

Notes

What was your biggest application point from your study on meditation? How will you incorporate what you learned into your life this week?

We saw that the psalmist meditates on the Word, but who does He say His teacher is?

Spend some time studying and considering what the New Testament says about God being our teacher. You may want to begin by listing some words to search in a concordance to bring you to the right neighborhoods! Record your findings below.

As you observed the Mem stanza did you notice the contrast between how the stanza opens and how it closes? Explain.

The psalmist opens with "O how I love Your law!" and closes with ". . . therefore I hate every false way." What are some false ways you recognize in your life and culture? If there are others you're not even aware of how might you learn to recognize them?

CONSIDER THIS:

Pointing to the True Teacher

Where does true wisdom come from? From the Word of God and the God of the Word. Human teachers simply point us to the true fountain of wisdom and help teach us how to drink for ourselves.

CONSIDER THIS:

Proverbs 6:16-19

"There are six things which the LORD hates,

Yes, seven which are an abomination to Him:

Haughty eyes, a lying tongue,

And hands that shed innocent blood,

A heart that devises wicked plans,

Feet that run rapidly to evil,

A false witness *who* utters lies,

And one who spreads strife among brothers."

Describe your relationship to God's Word today. Take a few minutes and write what's in your heart. Is the Word sweeter than chocolate to you? Is it sweeter than it used to be? Is it your delight or are you still asking God to give you more desire for His Word? Don't rush—take as much time as you need to think through these questions.

As we close out our study of the Mem stanza, take some time to meditate on the words of Psalm 119, quietly listening to God.

OBSERVE the TEXT of SCRIPTURE

READ the Nun stanza and mark every synonym for the Word of God. When you have done that,
record below what you learned from this stanza about God's Word.

נ

Nun

105   *Your word is a lamp to my feet and a light to my path.*

106   *I have sworn and I will confirm it, that I will keep Your righteous ordinances.*

107   *I am exceedingly afflicted; revive me, O LORD, according to Your word.*

108   *O accept the freewill offerings of my mouth, O LORD, and teach me Your ordinances.*

109   *My life is continually in my hand, yet I do not forget Your law.*

110   *The wicked have laid a snare for me, yet I have not gone astray from Your precepts.*

111   *I have inherited Your testimonies forever, for they are the joy of my heart.*

112   *I have inclined my heart to perform Your statutes forever, even to the end.*

DISCUSS with your GROUP or PONDER on your own . . .

What did you learn about the Word of God from the Nun stanza? Record your observations below.

What picture does the psalmist use to portray the Word in the opening line of this stanza?

In decisions you have to make every day, do you trust God when you can see only the next step? Do your actions align with your beliefs? Generally do you take the next step without assurance of what's coming down the path? Describe a time you stepped out with limited light on your path. Why did you act? What was the outcome?

If you are still dreaming of high beam headlights for your path, what steps can you take to begin conforming more fully to God's way? Prayerfully consider applications and record them below.

What attitude does the psalmist have in this stanza? What do you think of it?

FYI:

We Don't Drift into Devotion
"The idea of deliberate commitment is strong in this section. The verbs in 109, 110 express determination: 'I am determined not to forget,' 'not to stray'. We must not expect to drift by accident into devotion to the word!"[9]

—D.A. Carson in *New Bible Commentary*

Are you committed to remember God's Word and faithfulness to you? Is there anything in your commitment you need to address?

In the Nun stanza the psalmist pairs affliction and joy. How is your joy during times of affliction? How does the psalmist maintain his joy? As you answer, look for specific behaviors.

Notes

Week Four: **Are You Standing Firm in an Unsteady Culture?**

Do you have joy in your life? What does it typically depend on?

ONE STEP FURTHER:

Word Study: Joy

The testimonies of God are the joy of the psalmist's heart. If you have a little extra time this week, do a short study on the word *joy* and see what you can find out. Start by examining the Hebrew word used in Psalm 119:111. You may want to observe other words translated joy in the Old and New Testaments. Have fun!

Consider Psalm 16:11 as we bring a close to the Nun stanza:

You will make known to me the path of life;

In Your presence is fullness of joy;

In Your right hand there are pleasures forever.

TRUE STORIES:

Jeremiah's Joy in the Word

The prophet Jeremiah shares many similarities with the psalmist. He takes great joy in God's Word and is radically acquainted with suffering. Take some time this week to read and consider an excerpt from his life recorded in Jeremiah 15:15-21.

@THE END OF THE DAY . . .

Wisdom exceeding that of the aged and the teacher, guidance for the path of life, and a love for God's Word so alive it nearly breathes on its own. Who wouldn't want these? They are available to all who pursue God through His Word, and yet so few of us take full advantage of the bounty set before us.

What will it take for this to be your life? Spend as much time as you need considering this question before God as we close out our study for this week.

Week Five
Finding Security in Unstable Times

| Samekh | Ayin | Pe | Tsadhe |

God is a hiding place and shield to the psalmist who seeks and follows His Word. But not all seek His Word. Not all keep His Word. Some are double-minded. Some stray. Some oppress. In the midst of it all, the psalmist resolutely holds to his love for the Law, his hatred of every false way, and his belief in the wonder and treasure of God's Word. He actually believes that unfolding God's Word gives understanding to the simple. Just think . . . the psalmist is right!

AN OVERVIEW OF THE TEXT

OBSERVE the TEXT of SCRIPTURE

READ through Psalm 119 or meditate on a smaller part of it.

READ Psalm 119:113-144, the Samekh, Ayin, Pe, and Tsadhe stanzas, taking particular note of the contrast between those who follow God and those who don't.

Samekh

113   *I hate those who are double-minded, but I love Your law.*

114   *You are my hiding place and my shield; I wait for Your word.*

115   *Depart from me, evildoers, that I may observe the commandments of my God.*

116   *Sustain me according to Your word, that I may live; and do not let me be ashamed of my hope.*

117   *Uphold me that I may be safe, that I may have regard for Your statutes continually.*

118   *You have rejected all those who wander from Your statutes, for their deceitfulness is useless.*

119   *You have removed all the wicked of the earth like dross; therefore I love Your testimonies.*

120   *My flesh trembles for fear of You, and I am afraid of Your judgments.*

Ayin

121   *I have done justice and righteousness; do not leave me to my oppressors.*

122   *Be surety for Your servant for good; do not let the arrogant oppress me.*

123   *My eyes fail with longing for Your salvation and for Your righteous word.*

124   *Deal with Your servant according to Your lovingkindness and teach me Your statutes.*

125   *I am Your servant; give me understanding, that I may know Your testimonies.*

126   *It is time for the LORD to act, for they have broken Your law.*

127   *Therefore I love Your commandments above gold, yes, above fine gold.*

128   *Therefore I esteem right all Your precepts concerning everything, I hate every false way.*

Pe

129 *Your testimonies are wonderful; therefore my soul observes them.*

130 *The unfolding of Your words gives light; it gives understanding to the simple.*

131 *I opened my mouth wide and panted, for I longed for Your commandments.*

132 *Turn to me and be gracious to me, after Your manner with those who love Your name.*

133 *Establish my footsteps in Your word, and do not let any iniquity have dominion over me.*

134 *Redeem me from the oppression of man, that I may keep Your precepts.*

135 *Make Your face shine upon Your servant, and teach me Your statutes.*

136 *My eyes shed streams of water, because they do not keep Your law.*

Tsadhe

137 *Righteous are You, O LORD, and upright are Your judgments.*

138 *You have commanded Your testimonies in righteousness and exceeding faithfulness.*

139 *My zeal has consumed me, because my adversaries have forgotten Your words.*

140 *Your word is very pure, therefore Your servant loves it.*

141 *I am small and despised, yet I do not forget Your precepts.*

142 *Your righteousness is an everlasting righteousness, and Your law is truth.*

143 *Trouble and anguish have come upon me, yet Your commandments are my delight.*

144 *Your testimonies are righteous forever; give me understanding that I may live.*

Week Five: **Finding Security in Unstable Times**

DISCUSS with your GROUP or PONDER on your own . . .

What are your initial observations on the text?

What questions surface in your mind?

What key words and phrases can you focus on for further study?

OBSERVE the TEXT of SCRIPTURE

READ Samekh through Tsadhe (Psalm 119:113-144) again. This time compile a simple list of what you learn about the psalmist's adversaries. What characterizes them?

Looking over the list you compiled, in what specific ways does the psalmist differ? See if there are specific attitudes and actions in his life that kept him from similar behavior and actions.

What applications can you draw for your own life?

Week Five: **Finding Security in Unstable Times**

OBSERVE the TEXT of SCRIPTURE

READ the Samekh stanza and mark every synonym for the Word of God. When you have done that, record below what you learned from this stanza about God's Word.

Samekh

113   *I hate those who are double-minded, but I love Your law.*

114   *You are my hiding place and my shield; I wait for Your word.*

115   *Depart from me, evildoers, that I may observe the commandments of my God.*

116   *Sustain me according to Your word, that I may live; and do not let me be ashamed of my hope.*

117   *Uphold me that I may be safe, that I may have regard for Your statutes continually.*

118   *You have rejected all those who wander from Your statutes, for their deceitfulness is useless.*

119   *You have removed all the wicked of the earth like dross; therefore I love Your testimonies.*

120   *My flesh trembles for fear of You, and I am afraid of Your judgments.*

DISCUSS with your GROUP or PONDER on your own . . .

What did you learn from this stanza about God's Word?

The psalmist starts off the stanza with strong words about those who are double-minded. What does double-minded mean? Are people double-minded today?

Does this call to mind other references from Scripture? Can you think of examples of people in the Bible who were double-minded? If so, jot a couple of them down below and explain their stories.

Although there are many double-minded people in the Bible, we're going to focus on two cross references today that are especially relevant. The first, from the book of Joshua, is when the people of Israel were finally settling in the promised land. The second are the words of Jesus. As you read each of them, consider the temptations that cause double-mindedness and how similar situations may surface in your life.

Week Five: **Finding Security in Unstable Times**

Joshua 24

As you read this chapter, note the temptation facing the people of Israel as they enter the land. Is this still a temptation for us today? Explain your answer.

Within this chapter, Joshua says (v. 15): "If it is disagreeable in your sight to serve the LORD, choose for yourselves today whom you will serve: whether the gods which your fathers served which were
beyond the River, or the gods of the Amorites in whose land you are living; but as for me and my house, we will serve the LORD."

Israel had a choice to make and we know that although they all spoke the right words, many were far from God. Have you made a Joshua-like choice to follow God alone? What impact has your choice had on your life?

Matthew 6:16-34

In this passage, note how and where double-mindedness originates. Compare what Jesus tells His followers to seek versus what the world seeks. How much do you struggle with serving other masters? What other masters seek control of your life?

We have already spent some time looking at those who don't follow God. From this stanza, though, consider the benefit both the psalmist and his opponents had access to. How do we know they both had access? What have they done that shows us this?

TRUE STORIES:

Hesitating between two opinions . . .

The people of Israel had a history of double-mindedness regarding God and idols. If you have some extra time this week, read how the prophet Elijah dramatically called the people of Israel to make up their minds. You can read the account in 1 Kings 17–18.

Week Five: **Finding Security in Unstable Times**

Summarize the differences in how God relates to those who know Him and those who don't.

CONSIDER THIS:

Syncretism

Syncretism is the combining of beliefs or belief systems. Israel was almost always in trouble for combining God with the idols of the land. In what ways does syncretism show up in our culture and church today?

Digging Deeper

"My hiding place and my shield . . ."

This phrase is rich in meaning and comfort. As you have time this week, see what you can find out about it from cross references in Scripture as well as from other study tools you have access to. Record your findings below.

How can you apply your findings to specific events in your life?

FYI:

James 1:5-8

"But if any of you lacks wisdom, let him ask of God, who gives to all generously and without reproach, and it will be given to him. But he must ask in faith without any doubting, for the one who doubts is like the surf of the sea, driven and tossed by the wind. For that man ought not to expect that he will receive anything from the Lord, *being* a double-minded man, unstable in all his ways."

While the final verse of the stanza (119:120) focuses on fear, this is an appropriate response to a God who judges sin (cf. Matthew 10:28; Mark 9:43). In Christ we have been reconciled to a holy God who loves us. We must remember the loving God of Calvary is the holy God of Sinai. As we conclude our time in this stanza, consider the responses of those in the Bible who had direct encounters with God and see if they don't fit with the psalmist's assessment. If you're not sure where to look, take some time to read of Saul's encounter with Jesus on the road to Damascus (Acts 9) and the risen Christ's appearance to John (Revelation 1). Record your findings below.

ONE STEP FURTHER:

Word Study: Wait

If you have some extra time this week, take a closer look at the word translated "wait." Check out other ways it's translated and consider what waiting on God's word meant to the psalmist. How can we apply this to our lives today?

FYI:

2 Samuel 22:31

"As for God, His way is blameless;
The word of the LORD is tested;
He is a shield to all who take refuge in Him."

Read the rest of David's Song of Deliverance in 2 Samuel 22.

FYI:

Hebrews 12:28-29

"Therefore, since we receive a kingdom which cannot be shaken, let us show gratitude, by which we may offer to God an acceptable service with reverence and awe; for our God is a consuming fire."

Sweeter than Chocolate!®
An Inductive Study of Psalm 119

OBSERVE the TEXT of SCRIPTURE

READ the Ayin stanza and mark every synonym for the Word of God. When you have done that, record below what you learned from this stanza about God's Word.

Ayin

121   *I have done justice and righteousness; do not leave me to my oppressors.*

122   *Be surety for Your servant for good; do not let the arrogant oppress me.*

123   *My eyes fail with longing for Your salvation and for Your righteous word.*

124   *Deal with Your servant according to Your lovingkindness and teach me Your statutes.*

125   *I am Your servant; give me understanding, that I may know Your testimonies.*

126   *It is time for the LORD to act, for they have broken Your law.*

127   *Therefore I love Your commandments above gold, yes, above fine gold.*

128   *Therefore I esteem right all Your precepts concerning everything, I hate every false way.*

DISCUSS with your GROUP or PONDER on your own . . .

What did you learn from this stanza about God's Word?

Although we have looked at numerous questions and applications for each of the stanzas of Psalm 119, the Ayin stanza focuses on one statement that has vast implications for the way that we think as a society. In verse 128, the psalmist says, ***"Therefore I esteem right all* Your *precepts concerning everything . . . ."*** In a world of relativism and a culture of questioning all authority such as ours, this statement is as countercultural as they come.

What situation is the psalmist in as he esteems all God's precepts to be right? What is he up against? Is there any indication of how long he has been in his situation?

In verse 121 we see that the psalmist has "done justice and righteousness." What does He call on God to do and why?

Based on the text of this stanza, who does the psalmist deem to be in charge? Give some examples from the text to support your answer.

ONE STEP FURTHER:

Habakkuk

In a similar situation to the psalmist, the prophet Habakkuk calls out to God for justice against those who oppose His laws. You can read his story in the short book bearing his name. Record significant findings below.

Does the psalmist "know it all" about the Law of God? Explain your answer from the text.

CONSIDER THIS:

How much of the Bible is true?

How do you approach God's Word? Do you approach it assuming every last letter is true or do you approach it with skepticism? Even the slightest skepticism radically affects our views.

I work with the most wonderful Bible software in the world on a daily basis. The research it provides at my fingertips saves me hours every week. I have always trusted it without question. In a recent search, however, it returned some odd results and when I investigated further, I realized I had stumbled on a coding error. I never considered coding errors before . . . ever. Since then I have been watching everything with an eye toward error. I no longer assume that all its results will be flawless. The doubt has altered the way I interact with this software that I still entirely love.

But God's Word in its entirety is without error. When we side with the psalmist and esteem right all God's precepts concerning everything, we bring ourselves into proper submission to His Word.

Throughout this week, consider how much of God's Word you "esteem right." Record any reservations below.

Do you measure up with the psalmist's view of God's precepts? Do you esteem the whole Bible to be God's Word? What do others in our culture today think? What do they accept and reject?

If your life could use some improvement in this area, consider where your alignment may be off and how your life will change when you totally trust and esteem God's precepts to be right in every respect and at all times.

If you have doubts, bring them before the Lord today. He is big enough to handle your questions and your fears.

ONE STEP FURTHER:

Word Study: Esteem Right

Take some time and look at the Hebrew word translated "esteem right." Look at how it is used elsewhere in Scripture and see what scholars say about the way the psalmist viewed God's precepts. Record your findings below.

Week Five: **Finding Security in Unstable Times**

OBSERVE the TEXT of SCRIPTURE

READ the Pe stanza and mark every synonym for the Word of God. When you have done that, record below what you learned from this stanza about God's Word.

Pe

129   *Your testimonies are wonderful; therefore my soul observes them.*

130   *The unfolding of Your words gives light; it gives understanding to the simple.*

131   *I opened my mouth wide and panted, for I longed for Your commandments.*

132   *Turn to me and be gracious to me, after Your manner with those who love Your name.*

133   *Establish my footsteps in Your word, and do not let any iniquity have dominion over me.*

134   *Redeem me from the oppression of man, that I may keep Your precepts.*

135   *Make Your face shine upon Your servant, and teach me Your statutes.*

136   *My eyes shed streams of water, because they do not keep Your law.*

DISCUSS with your GROUP or PONDER on your own . . .

What did you learn from this stanza about God's Word?

As with everything, certain parts of this Psalm resonate with us more than others. They are words of hope to every person who has ever felt overwhelmed or under-brained. *The unfolding of Your words gives light; it gives understanding to the simple.*

   Satan would love to have you believe this isn't true. It's that simple. "Has God really said that His words give understanding to the simple?" It seems counterintuitive, but we serve a God who shows His strength in weak people and gives understanding to the simple.

As we consider the Pe stanza, let's investigate further this claim that the Word of God gives understanding to the simple. We're going to approach this question from two directions. First, take some time to search a concordance for the word translated "understanding." This will help us zero in on others in the Old Testament who had understanding. There are several notable characters including Joseph, David, Solomon, and Daniel. Focus on at least one of them and more if time permits. Read their stories and consider what the Word says about their wisdom. Also consider how they finished life. Did they end well or poorly? Record your findings below.

FYI:

Wonderful!
According to the *Theological Wordbook of the Old Testament*, the word translated "wonderful" means "unusual, beyond human capabilities."[11] In other words, it is something that shakes man and makes him take notice. It is the same root used to point to the coming child who will be called, among other titles, Wonderful Counselor (Isaiah 9:6).

Second, take some time to think through other examples including from the New Testament—understanding or wisdom showing up in unlikely people. One example you won't want to miss is that of Peter and John in Acts 4. What did the people notice about them? What was peculiar? Can the same be said of you?

What does the psalmist ask God for in this stanza?

Biblically speaking, does understanding insure that iniquity will not have dominion over us? Explain your answer. Cite chapter and verse.

Have you ever found yourself longing for God's commandments the way the psalmist does? Why or why not?

Digging Deeper

"My eyes shed streams of water . . ."

Throughout Psalm 119 we have seen from a number of angles the psalmist's view of those who do not follow God's laws—the path he walks. He has burning indignation, he seeks freedom from their oppression, and he hates the false way. In 119:136 we see another side: tears of grief over people who do not keep God's Law.

So here is the very wide open Digging Deeper mission: Spend some extended time in the Gospels this week examining how Jesus interacts with people who either do not know or do not keep God's Law. As you read, you'll notice that He deals in diverse ways. See if you can find patterns in the ways He deals with different types of people and attitudes. Record your findings and relevant applications below.

Is there anyone in your life who thinks the Word of God is too hard to understand? Spend some time talking with God and asking Him how you can winsomely bring to them the good news that God's Word is within reach–that our God gives understanding to the simple.

How can you live more consistently with the truth that God's Word gives understanding to the simple?

If you have questions or thoughts about the Pe stanza that are heavy on your heart, record them below.

ONE STEP FURTHER:

Word Study: *mitsvah / commandment*

What can you find out about *mitsvah* this week? How does it compare with synonyms we have seen so far? How is it typically used in Scripture?

FYI:

The Gospels

Matthew, Mark, Luke, and John, the first four books of the New Testament, are referred to as the Gospels (from the Greek word *euaggelion* meaning "good news").

OBSERVE the TEXT of SCRIPTURE

READ the Tsadhe stanza and mark every synonym for the Word of God. When you have done that, record below what you learned from this stanza about God's Word.

צ

Tsadhe

137   *Righteous are You, O LORD, and upright are Your judgments.*

138   *You have commanded Your testimonies in righteousness and exceeding faithfulness.*

139   *My zeal has consumed me, because my adversaries have forgotten Your words.*

140   *Your word is very pure, therefore Your servant loves it.*

141   *I am small and despised, yet I do not forget Your precepts.*

142   *Your righteousness is an everlasting righteousness, and Your law is truth.*

143   *Trouble and anguish have come upon me, yet Your commandments are my delight.*

144   *Your testimonies are righteous forever; give me understanding that I may live.*

DISCUSS with your GROUP or PONDER on your own . . .

What did you learn from this stanza about God's Word?

What does the psalmist say in this stanza about righteousness and what is righteous?

OBSERVE the TEXT of SCRIPTURE

READ 2 Corinthians 5:17-21 and note what Paul says about the righteousness of God.

17 *Therefore if anyone is in Christ, he is a new creature; the old things passed away; behold, new things have come.*

18 *Now all these things are from God, who reconciled us to Himself through Christ and gave us the ministry of reconciliation,*

19 *namely, that God was in Christ reconciling the world to Himself, not counting their trespasses against them, and He has committed to us the word of reconciliation.*

20 *Therefore, we are ambassadors for Christ, as though God were making an appeal through us; we beg you on behalf of Christ, be reconciled to God.*

21 *He made Him who knew no sin to be sin on our behalf, so that we might become the righteousness of God in Him.*

DISCUSS with your GROUP or PONDER on your own . . .

What does Paul say about the righteousness of God and how does it relate to us?

Week Five: **Finding Security in Unstable Times**

What does "new creature" mean to the way we live?

In the Pe stanza, we saw that the psalmist grieved over those who did not follow God's commandments. How does this compare with the Tsadhe stanza as the psalmist considers adversaries who have forgotten God's Words?

Does zeal for God and His Word ever consume you? What is it? Are all zealous behaviors pleasing to God? Explain.

Digging Deeper

"My zeal has consumed me"

The psalmist displays a zeal for the name and words of God. In your time of Digging Deeper this week, research and see if you can find some examples of people from the pages of Scripture who displayed godly zeal.

One character you won't want to miss is Phinehas. You will probably find him if you search a concordance. He's easy to overlook since he's not extremely well-known. Be sure to check out his story.

Another story in which a person displays a tremendous zeal for the Lord, which will not show up in a concordance search, is that of David and Goliath. If you don't know where it's located, search your concordance on Goliath and it will take you to the right neighborhood.

When you have finished your research, record your biggest application point.

ONE STEP FURTHER:

Righteousness
Take some time this week to examine the words used in the Old and New Testaments for *righteousness*. Record what you learn below.

@THE END OF THE DAY . . .

Can you believe that we only have one more week and four short stanzas to go?! Let's finish strong. As we close our study this week, spend some quiet time with God reflecting on the words of this Psalm and asking Him to regenerate your heart with the truths you most need at this hour. Indeed, if God is for us, who can be against us?!

Week Six
Ready for Every Tomorrow!

ק
Qoph

ר
Resh

שׁ
Shin

ת
Tav

Can you believe that we are on the final leg of our journey? We have taken many steps on our extended one-chapter tour. In order to allow us enough time to consider how we need to respond to what we have learned, we're going to look at the Qoph and Resh stanzas together and do the same for Shin and Tav. We're also going to be doing some read-throughs of the whole Psalm. So, make sure you begin early this week, not because there is more work but because of the kind of work it will be. Much of the time on this chapter will be spent not so much researching topics and writing out responses, but reflecting on precepts you have learned so far and considering how you can apply them in your own life. This will be a week of processing, meditating, and seeking God for answers of how to get what is in our heads and hearts out to our hands and feet.

A TIME of REVIEW

As we begin today, prayerfully read through the entire text of Psalm 119 and jot down your biggest application points so far. Application is not new knowledge you have gained. We're not talking about how you can apply what you have learned to your spouse, children, or next-door neighbor either. We're talking about changing how *you* think and act. How is God using His Word and Spirit to conform *you* to the image of His Son?

AN OVERVIEW OF THE TEXT

OBSERVE the TEXT of SCRIPTURE

READ Psalm 119:145-160 (the Qoph and Resh stanzas) and mark every synonym for the Word of God. When you have done that, record below what you learned from these stanzas about God's Word.

ק

Qoph

145 I cried with all my heart; answer me, O LORD! I will observe Your statutes.

146 I cried to You; save me and I shall keep Your testimonies.

147 I rise before dawn and cry for help; I wait for Your words.

148 My eyes anticipate the night watches, that I may meditate on Your word.

149 Hear my voice according to Your lovingkindness; revive me, O LORD, according to Your ordinances.

150 Those who follow after wickedness draw near; they are far from Your law.

151 You are near, O LORD, and all Your commandments are truth.

152 Of old I have known from Your testimonies that You have founded them forever.

ר

Resh

153 Look upon my affliction and rescue me, for I do not forget Your law.

154 Plead my cause and redeem me; revive me according to Your word.

155 Salvation is far from the wicked, for they do not seek Your statutes.

156 Great are Your mercies, O LORD; revive me according to Your ordinances.

157 Many are my persecutors and my adversaries, yet I do not turn aside from Your testimonies.

158 I behold the treacherous and loathe them, because they do not keep Your word.

159 Consider how I love Your precepts; revive me, O LORD, according to Your lovingkindness.

160 The sum of Your word is truth, and every one of Your righteous ordinances is everlasting.

Week Six: **Ready for Every Tomorrow!**

DISCUSS with your GROUP or PONDER on your own . . .

What are your initial observations on the text?

What questions surface in your mind?

What words and phrases might you focus on for further study?

What's the psalmist's situation in the Qoph and Resh stanzas? How does he respond? Is it consistent with his responses in previous stanzas?

Read through Qoph and Resh again looking for references to time and proximity. First let's consider time. When does the psalmist pursue God? What kind of attitude does he pursue with?

How does this compare with your pursuing with respect to both time and intensity?

QUIZ:

The Whole Alphabet
(Open book if you need it!)
Without looking, try writing the names of all 22 stanzas of Psalm 119 and the corresponding Hebrew letters.

1.

2.

3.

4.

5.

6.

7.

8.

9.

10.

11.

12.

13.

14.

15.

16.

17.

18.

19.

20.

21.

22.

Sweeter than Chocolate!®
An Inductive Study of Psalm 119

What seems to fuel the psalmist's intensity? Read closely for more than one possibility. Explain your answer(s).

ONE STEP FURTHER:

The Nearness of God

This week, practice considering and contemplating the nearness of God. Consider your place in the body of Christ and what that means to your relationship with God and others in Christ's body. Think through the ramifications for living humbly in harmony with one another.

When circumstances get ugly, is your tendency to press into God or pull away from God? Why?

FYI:

Qadam

147 I rise (qadam) before dawn and cry for help; I wait for Your words.

148 My eyes anticipate (qadam) the night watches, that I may meditate on Your word.

Both the word "rise" in verse 147 and "anticipate" in 148 are translations of the Hebrew word *qadam.* The psalmist is eager for God's Word. He gets up early for it and redeems the night watches as well.

To what degree do you eagerly anticipate your time with God in His Word?

What did you observe with regard to words that mean proximity? Who is near? Who is far? What picture is being painted?

Have you experienced the reviving power of God's Word in your life? Explain.

ONE STEP
FURTHER:

Word Study: Revive
The Hebrew word translated "revive" in both the Qoph and Resh stanzas occurs frequently throughout Psalm 119. If you have some extra time this week, examine the Hebrew word and record what you learn below.

Digging Deeper

The Sum of Your Word is Truth

The psalmist closes the Resh stanza with the line, "The sum of Your word is truth, and every one of Your righteous ordinances is everlasting." As time permits, consider where Scripture speaks of itself and what it says. What, for example, is Jesus' view of Scripture? Paul's view? Peter's view?

OBSERVE the TEXT of SCRIPTURE

READ Psalm 161-176 (the Shin and Tav stanzas). Mark every synonym for the Word of God. When you have done that, record below what you learned from these stanzas about God's Word.

Shin

161 *Princes persecute me without cause, but my heart stands in awe of Your words.*

162 *I rejoice at Your word, as one who finds great spoil.*

163 *I hate and despise falsehood, but I love Your law.*

164 *Seven times a day I praise You, because of Your righteous ordinances.*

165 *Those who love Your law have great peace, and nothing causes them to stumble.*

166 *I hope for Your salvation, O LORD, and do Your commandments.*

167 *My soul keeps Your testimonies, and I love them exceedingly.*

168 *I keep Your precepts and Your testimonies, for all my ways are before You.*

Tav

169 *Let my cry come before You, O LORD; give me understanding according to Your word.*

170 *Let my supplication come before You; deliver me according to Your word.*

171 *Let my lips utter praise, for You teach me Your statutes.*

172 *Let my tongue sing of Your word, for all Your commandments are righteous.*

173 *Let Your hand be ready to help me, for I have chosen Your precepts.*

174 *I long for Your salvation, O LORD, and Your law is my delight.*

175 *Let my soul live that it may praise You, and let Your ordinances help me.*

176 *I have gone astray like a lost sheep; seek Your servant, for I do not forget Your commandments.*

DISCUSS with your GROUP or PONDER on your own . . .

What are your initial observations on the text?

What questions surface in your mind?

What words and phrases can you focus on for further study?

In looking at Shin and Tav together, are they similar? Different? What is the focus of each?

ONE STEP FURTHER:

John 1

If you have a little time this week, do some side reading in the Gospel of John and the First Letter of John. Having spent so much time with the psalmist looking at the Word of God, you will so appreciate the words of the evangelist. Note what you discover below.

In both Shin and Tav, the psalmist looks eagerly for something. He hopes for it in Shin and longs for it in Tav. Use your study tools to locate the Hebrew word. When you have found it, record it below. Then go to the New Testament and see if you can find out what the name "Jesus" means. Do you see the significance?

What extremely practical benefits does the Shin stanza present?

Do you experience peace in your life? Do you perceive it in people around you? When you experience peace, what characterizes your thinking? Think about a time you lacked peace and describe your thinking then.

Do you ever fear messing up your life? What does the psalmist say about stumbling? Where else does the Word of God address this issue? Is the message consistent? What is the reasoning behind the assurances given?

How will the way you live change when you grasp this truth?

THINK ON THIS:

Don't be a Lancelot

My all-time favorite musical is Lerner and Lowes' *Camelot.* It is the tragic story of a king with a vision of a better world and his devoted but self-righteous knight who ends up bringing down the kingdom when he falls into temptation with his beloved king's wife. What does this have to do with Bible study? Lancelot personifies a way of thinking we can easily imitate if we fail to doggedly and persistently fix our eyes on Jesus. He was a great knight but righteous in his own eyes and he fell into the trap described so succinctly in Proverbs 16:18: "Pride goes before destruction, and a haughty spirit before stumbling."

Week Six: **Ready for Every Tomorrow!**

Having studied 175 verses of the psalmist's devotion to God and His Law, what do you make of verse 176?

Take some time to carefully read Luke 15:1-7 and reflect on its relationship to Psalm 119.

For all the psalmist's devotion and love for God, he still needed a Savior . . . and His faithful God indeed sent Jesus on a mission to seek and to save the lost.

Sweeter than Chocolate!®

An Inductive Study of Psalm 119

Digging Deeper

The Law that Points to Jesus

If you have some extra time on your hands this week, research the ways Moses and the Law point to Jesus. If you have a blank look on your face right now or don't have adequate time, don't sweat it. Just move on to the final application questions and leave this for another day.

TRUE STORIES:

Zaccheus, Luke 19:1-10
As you read the story of the "wee little man," take special note of the last two verses. Record what you learn below.

HEAD, HEART, HANDS, and FEET

Seeing God's Words move from our mind and will to our hands and feet is critically important. Why? Well, for one thing it's a really, really big deal to Jesus. Check out His words in the Gospel of Matthew regarding the Pharisees who talked a good religious game but didn't live it out:

Then Jesus spoke to the crowds and to His disciples, saying: "The scribes and the Pharisees have seated themselves in the chair of Moses; therefore all that they tell you, do and observe, but do not do according to their deeds; for they say things *and do not do* them. *They tie up heavy burdens and lay them on men's shoulders, but they themselves are unwilling to move them with* so much as *a finger. But they do all their deeds to be noticed by men; for they broaden their phylacteries and lengthen the tassels* of their garments. *They love the place of honor at banquets and the chief seats in the synagogues, and respectful greetings in the market places, and being called Rabbi by men. But do not call* anyone *on earth your father; for One is your Father, He who is in heaven. Do not be called leaders; for One is your Leader,* that is, *Christ. But the greatest among you shall be your servant. Whoever exalts himself shall be humbled; and whoever humbles himself shall be exalted."*

–Matthew 23:1-12

As we began this week's study, we looked at the whole of Psalm 119 and recorded the application points God has been working in us. You may have had one, you may have had 176 or any number in between. Right now let's revisit the concept of specific application again. This time, though, we are going to get even more specific.

Read through Psalm 119 again over the next day or two and ask God to show you one priority area of application, one place where you can intentionally submit to His Spirit to align your life more with His Word. As you consider this, think in terms of specifics, not generalities.

For example, many of us know we should eat better. That's *general*. A *specific* application is "I will eat three servings of vegetables a day." General is "I should exercise more." Specific is "I'll walk for 30 minutes three times a week."

Here is a specific application from Psalm 119:

When I am tempted to worry, I will instead meditate on God's Word by recalling and considering attributes of God like His sovereignty and goodness, by seeking His help through prayer, and by bringing specific Scripture passages to bear on worrisome situations. I will prepare in advance by investigating passages that address the topic of worry, and I will ask God to help me to be aware when I am beginning to worry and incline my heart toward Him and His Word.

Take some time to think through this, perhaps talking with a trusted friend or mentor, and jot down your thoughts remembering always that whatever good we do is the work of God's Spirit who empowers us to walk in His ways.

Take some time to identify questions you either didn't or couldn't answer.

Does something you learned about God or His Word from Psalm 119 thrill you? A truth, perhaps, that you will begin to live more and more in light of and bring to bear increasingly in the tough situations of life? If so, record it as briefly as possible below. Why briefly? The shorter it is, the more likely you will be able to remember it.

Week Six: **Ready for Every Tomorrow!**

@THE END OF THE DAY . . .

It is my deep hope that you have gained at least a beginning knowledge of Psalm 119 over our past six weeks together so that you are equipped to walk more and more on the path God intends for you. It is also my hope that you will not think that because you invested some time that you now have this text in your back pocket. For all our digging, we have only begun to scratch the surface. We are like archaeologists who have dug in our little plot of ground, uncovered great treasures, but who sit on a find that exceeds our wildest expectations. Although we have seen gems in God's Word, we cannot even begin to imagine what He has in store for us and for those who seek Him. This should move us to humility, wonder, and eager expectation!

I am so thrilled that you have stayed the course and finished this study on Psalm 119! God's Words through the psalmist are words of wisdom, healing, guidance, endurance, and instruction. They are words to be prayed, meditated on, and lived out as we love God, His Word, and people in the everydayness of life.

Now the God of peace, who brought up from the dead the great Shepherd of the sheep through the blood of the eternal covenant, even Jesus our Lord, equip you in every good thing to do His will, working in us that which is pleasing in His sight, though Jesus Christ, to whom be the glory forever and ever. Amen.

—Hebrews 13:20-21

Works Cited

1   Vlach, Ph.D., Michael J. "Americans and the Bible: Bible Ownership, Reading, Study and Knowledge in the United States." Theologicalstudies.org. <http://theologicalstudies.org>

2   Harris, R. L., Gleason L. Archer, and Bruce K. Waltke. Theological Wordbook of the Old Testament. New York: Moody, 2003, Volume 2, page 904.

3   Hebrew-English Tanakh. Washington D.C.: Jewish Publication Society, 2003, page 1564

4   Tozer, A. W. Knowledge of the Holy. New York: Harper San Francisco, 1978.

5   "Pericope - Definition from the Merriam-Webster Online Dictionary." Dictionary and Thesaurus - Merriam-Webster Online. 06 Jan. 2009 <http://www.merriam-webster.com/dictionary/pericope>.

6   Freeman, James M. The New Manners and Customs of the Bible. Ed. Harold J. Chadwick. New York: Bridge-Logos, 1998.

7   Logos Bible Software. Vers. Scholar Silver. Computer software. Logos Research Systems, Inc. Bellingham, WA.

8   Carmichael, Amy. Candles in the Dark. Danbury: Christian Literature Crusade, Incorporated, 1982.

9   Motyer, J. A., Gordon J. Wenham, and Donald A. Carson, eds. New Bible Commentary. New York: InterVarsity P, 1994.

10 Harris, R. L., Gleason L. Archer, and Bruce K. Waltke. Theological Wordbook of the Old Testament. New York: Moody, 2003, Volume 1, page 100.

11 Harris, R. L., Gleason L. Archer, and Bruce K. Waltke. Theological Wordbook of the Old Testament. New York: Moody, 2003, Volume 2, page 723.

RESOURCES

Helpful Study Tools

The New How to Study Your Bible
Eugene, Oregon: Harvest House
Publishers

The New Inductive Study Bible
Eugene, Oregon: Harvest House
Publishers

Logos Bible Software
Available at www.logos.com

Greek Word Study Tools

Kittel, G., Friedrich, G., & Bromiley,
G.W.
*Theological Dictionary of the New
Testament, Abridged* (also known as
Little Kittel)
Grand Rapids, Michigan: W.B.
Eerdmans Publishing Company

Zodhiates, Spiros
*The Complete Word Study Dictionary:
New Testament*
Chattanooga, Tennessee: AMG
Publishers

Hebrew Word Study Tools

Harris, R.L., Archer, G.L., & Walker,
B.K.
*Theological Wordbook of the Old
Testament* (also known as TWOT)
Chicago, Illinois: Moody Press

Zodhiates, Spiros
*The Complete Word Study Dictionary:
Old Testament*
Chattanooga, Tennessee: AMG
Publishers

General Word Study Tools

Strong, James
*The New Strong's Exhaustive
Concordance of the Bible*
Nashville, Tennessee: Thomas Nelson

Recommended Commentary Sets

Expositor's Bible Commentary
Grand Rapids, Michigan: Zondervan

NIV Application Commentary
Grand Rapids, Michigan: Zondervan

The New American Commentary
Nashville, Tennessee: Broadman and
Holman Publishers

One-Volume Biblical Commentary

Carson, D.A.
*New Bible Commentary: 21st Century
Edition* (4th ed.)
Leicester, England; Downers Grove, IL:
InterVarsity Press

ABOUT PRECEPT

Precept Ministries International was raised up by God for the sole purpose of establishing people in God's Word to produce reverence for Him. It serves as an arm of the church without respect to denomination. God has enabled Precept to reach across denominational lines without compromising the truths of His inerrant Word. We believe every word of the Bible was inspired and given to man as all that is necessary for him to become mature and thoroughly equipped for every good work of life. This ministry does not seek to impose its doctrines on others, but rather to direct people to the Master Himself, who leads and guides by His Spirit into all truth through a systematic study of His Word. The ministry produces a variety of Bible studies and holds conferences and intensive Training Workshops designed to establish attendees in the Word through Inductive Bible Study.

Jack Arthur and his wife, Kay, founded Precept Ministries in 1970. Kay and the ministry staff of writers produce **Precept Upon Precept** studies, **In & Out** studies, **Lord** series studies, the **New Inductive Study Series** studies, **40-Minute** studies, and **Discover 4 Yourself Inductive Bible Studies for Kids**. From years of diligent study and teaching experience, Kay and the staff have developed these unique, inductive courses that are used in nearly 150 countries and 70 languages.

MOBILIZING

We are mobilizing believers who "rightly handle the Word of God" and want to use their spiritual gifts and skills to reach 10 million more people with Inductive Bible Study by 2015. If you share our passion for establishing people in God's Word, we invite you to find out more. Visit **www.precept.org/Mobilize** for more detailed information.

ANSWERING THE CALL

Now that you've studied and prayerfully considered the scriptures, is there something new for you to believe or do, or did it move you to make a change in your life? It's one of the many amazing and supernatural results of being in His life-changing Word—God speaks to us. At Precept Ministries International, we believe that we have heard God speak about our part in the Great Commission. He has told us in His Word to make disciples by teaching people how to study His Word. We plan to reach 10 million more people with Inductive Bible Study in the next five years. If you share our passion for establishing people in God's Word, we invite you to join us! Will you prayerfully consider giving monthly to the ministry? We've done the math and estimate that for every $2 you give, we can reach one person with life-changing Inductive Bible Study. If you give online at **www.precept.org/ATC**, we save on administrative costs so that your dollars go farther. And if you give monthly as an online recurring gift, fewer dollars go into administrative costs and more go toward ministry.

Please pray about how the Lord might lead you to answer the call.

Sweeter than Chocolate!®

PAM GILLASPIE

Pam Gillaspie, a passionate Bible student and teacher, authors Precept's *Sweeter than Chocolate!*® and *Cookies on the Lower Shelf*™ Bible study series. Pam holds a BA in Biblical Studies from Wheaton College in Wheaton, Illinois. She and her husband live in suburban Chicago, Illinois with their son, daughter, and Great Dane. Her greatest joy is encouraging others to read God's Word widely and study it deeply . . . precept upon precept.

Connect with Pam at:

www.deepandwide.org

 pamgillaspie

 pamgillaspie